On Western Terrorism

CHOMSKY PERSPECTIVES*

After the Cataclysm:
The Political Economy of Human Rights – Volume II

Culture of Terrorism

The Fateful Triangle:
The United States, Israel, and the Palestinians

On Power and Ideology:
The Managua Lectures

Pirates and Emperors, Old and New:
International Terrorism in the Real World

Powers and Prospects:
Reflections on Human Nature and the Social Order

Propaganda and the Public Mind:
Interviews by David Barsamian

Rethinking Camelot:
JFK, the Vietnam War, and US Political Culture

Rogue States:
The Rule of Force in World Affairs

Turning the Tide:
U.S. Intervention in Central America and the Struggle for Peace

The Washington Connection and Third World Fascism:
The Political Economy of Human Rights – Volume I

Year 501:
The Conquest Continues

* not for sale in North America

On Western Terrorism

From Hiroshima to Drone Warfare

NEW EDITION

Noam Chomsky and Andre Vltchek

PlutoPress
www.plutobooks.com

First published 2013; new edition 2017 by Pluto Press
345 Archway Road, London N6 5AA

This edition not for sale in Canada

www.plutobooks.com

British Library Cataloguing in Publication Data
A catalogue record for this book is available from the British Library

ISBN   978 0 7453 9931 7   Paperback
ISBN   978 1 7868 0072 5   PDF eBook
ISBN   978 1 7868 0074 9   Kindle eBook
ISBN   978 1 7868 0073 2   EPUB eBook

This book is printed on paper suitable for recycling and made from fully
managed and sustained forest sources. Logging, pulping and manufacturing
processes are expected to conform to the environmental standards of the
country of origin.

Typeset by Stanford DTP Services, Northampton, England

Simultaneously printed in the United Kingdom and United States of America

Contents

Preface to the Second Edition

Noam Chomsky

Our discussions of Western terrorism went to press shortly after the French-British-U.S. attack on Libya—in violation of the resolution rammed through the UN Security Council by the imperial triumvirate and dismissing the continuing efforts of the African Union to pursue diplomatic paths that could have averted the disaster that ensued (122f.).

At the time, Western leaders were hailing the assault as a "historic victory for the people of Libya" with NATO's help (Ivo Daalder, U.S. permanent representative to NATO, and James Stavridis, supreme allied commander of Europe) in which the U.S. "achieved our objectives" without putting a single pair of boots on the ground (President Obama).

In the real world, "NATO's intervention appears to have increased the violent death toll more than tenfold," according to an analysis by Alan Kuperman in the main establishment journal, *Foreign Affairs*, while devastating the country and leaving it in the hands of warring militias. The assault also shifted Libyan exports from oil to a huge flood of weapons and jihadis, mostly to West Africa, which is now the major center of radical Islamist terror according to UN statistics, while providing ISIS with a new foothold in Africa.

The triumph is fairly typical of the "global war on terror" that was declared in September 2001 by President George W. Bush—to be more accurate, re-declared; 20 years earlier, President Reagan had declared a war on international terror, "the plague of the modern age," a war that quickly turned into a murderous terrorist war, primarily targeting popular uprisings in Central America that sought to free themselves from brutal U.S.-backed dictatorships. Hundreds of thousands were killed, overwhelmingly by forces armed and trained by Washington. Meanwhile Reagan was also the last supporter of terrorist forces in Southern Africa allied with the apartheid regime in South Africa. All best forgotten.

At the time of Bush's re-declaration of the war, radical Islamic terror was localized in small tribal regions at the Afghan–Pakistan border. By now it is all over the world. Each blow of the sledgehammer spreads the plague, just as expected when immediate resort to violence displaces available peaceful means while the roots of the problems are ignored.

Meanwhile, President Obama opened new chapters in terrorism with his global assassination campaign, targeting people suspected of intending to harm the U.S., often on the flimsiest evidence. The *New York Times* reported that the government was counting "all military-age males [killed] in a strike zone" as combatants, though they might be "posthumously" proven innocent by "explicit intelligence." U.S. Ambassador to Pakistan Cameron Munter hardly exaggerated when he informed the press that the definition of a legitimate target is "a male between the ages of 20 and 40."

By 2016, Obama expanded his terrorist campaign to many countries. In the early months of the year, strikes killed people in Yemen, Syria, northern Iraq, Afghanistan and Somalia, in the last case 150 suspected militants at what was claimed to be a training camp for terrorists. Unknown numbers are "collateral damage." Their murder is often anticipated, as when the CIA attacked a crowd of some 5,000 mourners at the funeral of a mid-ranking Taliban commander in June 2009, killing a reported 83 people, 45 of them civilians, including ten children.

The terror goes far beyond assassination. A study of drone warfare by Stanford and New York University law schools reports that:

> Their presence terrorizes men, women, and children, giving rise to anxiety and psychological trauma among civilian communities. Those living under drones have to face the constant worry that a deadly strike may be fired at any moment, and the knowledge that they are powerless to protect themselves. These fears have affected behavior. The US practice of striking one area multiple times, and evidence that it has killed rescuers, makes both community members and humanitarian workers afraid or unwilling to assist injured victims. Some community members shy away from gathering in groups, including important tribal dispute-resolution bodies, out of fear that they may attract the attention of drone operators.*

The Middle East region has changed in many ways since the first edition of this book was published. ISIS, another monstrous outcome of the Iraq invasion, had not yet appeared. The Arab Spring had not yet turned into the nightmare of the

---

* *Living Under Drones: Death, Injury, and Trauma to Civilians From US Drone Practices in Pakistan*, September 2012, p. vii.

Egyptian dictatorship and, worst of all, the horrendous Syrian catastrophe. The "refugee crisis"—more accurately, a moral crisis of the West—had not yet reached its shocking scale and character. And critical developments were underway elsewhere in the world that there is no space to review here, but that bear on the general theme of the discussions in this book.

Noam Chomsky
October 3, 2016

Introduction

Andre Vltchek

Could the man with whom I debated the state of our world be described as "the greatest intellectual of the twentieth century," or "the most quoted person of our time," or a courageous warrior against injustice and against the ravishment of billions of defenseless men, women, and children all over the world? He could, of course, but he would not appreciate grand words and celebratory slogans.

To me, Noam Chomsky is a man who also loves roses, who enjoys a good glass of wine, and who can speak with great warmth and tenderness about the past, about the people who crossed his path in so many places of our planet; a man who knows how to ask questions and who then attentively listens to answers; a very kind person, a caring human being, and a dear friend.

To one of the walls of Noam's office at MIT is attached an iconic photo of, and a quote by, Bertrand Russell: "Three passions, simple but overwhelmingly strong have governed my life: the longing for love, the search for knowledge, and unbearable pity for the suffering of mankind."

For some reason, whenever I remember these words, it always feels that Noam uttered them. Maybe because he acts as if they represent his own philosophy of life.

* * *

"Let's take a walk," Noam told me many years ago, as we met, for the first time, face to face, in New York City. "And let me buy you a coffee," he teased me. "I am a rich American, you know..."

We grabbed two coffees at a local deli and set on the bench, for hours in the park, near New York University. We talked, we "exchanged notes," and we discussed the world. Of course I was also holding U.S. citizenship, but Noam was truly a "rich American" in this little game of ours, Noam of all people!

From the first moments I spent with him, I felt kindness and camaraderie; I felt at ease, as if the age gap did not exist, as if I would be meeting an old friend, not one of the greatest contemporary thinkers.

By then we had our history; we corresponded for several years—about politics and the crimes committed by the West, but also about much simpler things, like our passion for knowledge and where it really began. In his case, one of the catalysts was that famous newsstand above the subway stop on Broadway and 72nd Street, which was owned by Noam's relatives. In my case, it was my Russian grandmother who began reading to me countless great books when I was hardly four years old.

Noam wrote to me a lot about his family, about how it was growing up in the United States, about his daughter who then lived in Nicaragua, and about his beloved wife—Carol—who was also very kind to me, reading my early political writings, and offering her warm and heartfelt support and encouragement. "Carol had no choice but to become a great linguist and professor. You know, someone had to support the family, and I was constantly in jail," explained Noam in one of his emails, remembering Vietnam War era.

I wrote to him about my own childhood, which had been complex and often unsettling, a result of growing up in a mixed race family: with an Asian and Russian mother and European father. We shared many things, and it was not about our work, only: to me Noam had been like a close relative, a paternal figure that had been so desperately lacking in my own life; but also an example of courage, of brilliance and integrity.

*　*　*

While Noam was relentlessly traveling, visiting places and people that were in need of his attention and support, at some point I decided to return to my work in war zones, to go back to the conflict areas, where extermination of millions of human beings had been constantly going on, for decades, centuries.

People were dying; they were being slaughtered in the name of freedom and democracy and other lofty slogans, but slaughtered nevertheless. I was witnessing—writing about, filming and photographing—so many horrors and broken lives, events that are often too difficult, too painful to describe. But I felt I had to do it, in order to know, to understand, to offer testimonies from "marginal places"; accounts so rare at this time and age.

The great majority of events that were causing the suffering of countless human beings all over the world were related to greed, to the desire to rule and to control, coming almost exclusively from both the "old continent" and its powerful but ruthless offspring on the other shore of the Atlantic. The cause could have many different names—colonialism or neo-colonialism, imperialism or corporate greed—but the name does not really matter, as it is only suffering that does.

I felt the greatest respect and admiration for Noam's work, but I never wanted to follow him. I wanted to complement his efforts. While he was engaged on the intellectual and activist fronts, I tried to amass evidence from the combat zones, from the "crime scenes," evidence both verbal and visual.

What he has been doing could not be done better; could hardly be more effective. There was no point copying and reconfirming what Noam Chomsky was already doing so brilliantly.

Instead, I went to the Democratic Republic of Congo and Rwanda, to Uganda and Egypt, to Israel, Palestine, Indonesia, Timor Leste, Oceania and so many other places that had fallen victim to plunder, humiliation and carnage, either performed by or orchestrated in Western capitals. I was trying to illustrate, independently, what he was saying and describing.

For many years, Noam and I were exchanging and comparing notes. Sometimes it was done frequently, sometimes with long pauses, but it was always done, diligently. The way I saw it, we were fighting for the same cause, for the right of self-determination and real freedom for all people around the world. And we were fighting against colonialism and fascism, in whichever form it came.

We never pronounced these words, and were never seeking any definitions for our activities. For Noam, fighting injustice seemed to be as natural as breathing. For me, it became both a great honor and great adventure to work with him and to create images and reports inspired by his conclusions.

*　　*　　*

After witnessing and analyzing numerous atrocious conflicts, invasions and wars on all continents, I became convinced that almost all of them were orchestrated or provoked by Western geopolitical and economic interests. And the "information" about those murderous events and about the fate of human beings whom the colonial empires have been exterminating and sacrificing with very little thought, was grotesquely limited and twisted.

People residing outside Europe, the United States and a select few Asian countries had been described by George Orwell as "un-people," an expression that Noam also likes to use, sarcastically. At closer examination it becomes crystal clear that billions of "un-people" are actually the majority of the human race.

What I read in the Western press and what I witnessed all over the world somehow did not match. Failed feudal states were hailed as "vibrant democracies," oppressive religious regimes were described as "tolerant" and "moderate" countries, while nationalist and socially-oriented states were incessantly demonized, their indigenous and alternative development and social models vilified and portrayed in the bleakest colors imaginable.

Brilliant propagandists in London and Washington made sure to "protect" the public all over the world from "uncomfortable truths." Public opinion, ideology and perceptions were manufactured. And like mass-produced cars or smartphones, they were marketed through advertisement and propaganda.

Noam has written several books and on the propaganda role of the mass media, essential to understanding how our world has been controlled and governed. I have also written countless reports, giving examples of ideological manipulation by the Western powers and their institutions, often addressing issues like propaganda and mass-media manipulation.

Western misinformation has been clearly targeting countries that have been refusing to succumb to Western dictate: Cuba and Venezuela, Eritrea and China, Iran, Zimbabwe, Russia, while glorifying those nations that were either ravishing its neighbors on behalf of Western interests, or plundering their own impoverished people: Rwanda, Uganda, Kenya, Indonesia, Saudi Arabia, Israel, the Philippines and many others.

Fear and nihilism have proliferated all over the world. It was the fear of being targeted, of being "punished" by the seemingly omnipotent Western masters of the world. It was the fear of being labeled, sidelined, or marked.

Nihilism has also been spread by propagandists firmly entrenched in Western media outlets and in academia. It has been disseminated through propaganda apparatchiks, who were hired to target all progressive and independent ideas and ideals coming in different forms and from all corners of the world. Optimism, zeal, as well as all dreams for better arrangement of the world, have been attacked, poisoned, discredited, or at least ridiculed.

* * *

I often felt desperate, but I was never ready to give up the fight. Too much was at stake and personal exhaustion appeared to be irrelevant.

Circling the world, working day and night on my films and books, I was often thinking about Noam. He was the most stable, the most intellectually and morally reliable human being that I knew. And his dedication, his courage to stand tall and proud "facing the tanks" of the Empire was both encouraging and inspiring. At one point I felt the burning desire to join forces with him and to summarize, through dialogue, what I learned about the unsettling state of our world.

I wrote to him, asking him to spend at least two days discussing our world in front of the film cameras. He generously agreed. His magnificent but protective assistant, Bev, gave her kind blessing. It was happening! My Japanese film editor, Hata Takeshi, and I quickly agreed to co-produce the film version of our conversation. My London-based publisher, Pluto Press, decided to issue our conversation in a book form. Everything was suddenly moving at lightning speed.

No money was raised. Hata-san brought to Boston a small but highly professional team of Japanese filmmakers which, realizing the importance of the project, asked for no advance financial compensation, acting on the abstract promise of future reimbursement.

I flew from Africa to Europe and from there to Santiago de Chile, embarking on a long journey from Temuco to Boston, where my encounter with Noam was going to take place. I was collecting film footage as I went, traveling though the countries of Latin America that for many years were once my home; the countries that were earlier devastated by imperialism, but were now liberated and suddenly full of optimism and colors, openly socialist and free.

Yayoi flew to Boston from Kenya, to offer her support and help. Our Boston-based friend, Fotini, helped with both lodging and transportation. The film crew arrived two days before the meeting. Everything was working.

*   *   *

For two days, for many hours, at MIT, we debated the responsibility of Western nations for the countless onslaughts, and for centuries of terror, that they spread all over the world.

Despite the topic—so painful and poignant—the conversation flowed easily and freely.

It was not that we agreed on every issue: Noam appeared to be more optimistic about the Arab Spring and the situation in Turkey than I was. And, unlike me, he appeared to be convinced that the West was finally losing its grip on the rest of the world. But we shared all essential values, and the discussion was that of two close allies joining forces in a struggle for the same cause.

1 Noam Chomsky and Andre Vltchek in conversation in Chomsky's office in MIT, June 14, 2012. (Copyright Yayoi Segi)

The topics in our conversation ranged, as the title of this book suggests, from Hiroshima to drone warfare, from the early days of colonialism to modern methods that are used by the Western propaganda apparatus. But this exchange also brought us back to that newsstand at 72nd Street and Broadway in New York City. It took us to Nicaragua and Cuba, to China, Chile and Istanbul, to so many places that are dear to us.

I launched our discussion by declaring that, according to my calculation; around 55 million people were killed directly after the end of World War II, as a result of Western imperialism. Hundreds of millions were slaughtered indirectly. And we concluded our discussion when Noam declared that one always has a choice: to do something about the situation, or to do nothing.

* * *

For several months after the conversation, I circled the globe, collecting footage for the film, and images for our book. I wanted to illustrate what we were saying, to get our viewers and readers involved through our words, but also through the visuals. For weeks I was sharing hopes and dreams with Egyptian revolutionaries in Cairo and in Port Said, I was also sharing frustration with gentle Druze inhabitants of the Syrian Golan Heights occupied by Israel; I was photographing and filming at several conflict areas in Africa, Oceania, and Asia.

Noam was correct: it was easy to give up and declare that nothing can be done. It was easy to shout at a television set, to say that the struggle has been lost. But then, nothing would ever change. And there were so many things that had to be changed, in order for the mankind to survive and to prosper. The alternative is to work day and night for substantial changes, to fight for those changes. It is more difficult, but also much more rewarding.

The journey: marked with both work and the struggle, was breathtaking. What we were doing was not a sacrifice; it was both a joy and privilege. By the time our conversation took place, I had known Noam for more than 15 years. It was a great honor to be acquainted with him, to work with him, and to learn from him directly.

After we parted, life threw me, again and again, to the battlefields and conflict zones. I often thought about Noam, about all that had been said. And in my mind, I have often been consulting him. When things got rough, I developed a habit of recalling the motto which hangs in Noam's office: "Three passions, simple but overwhelmingly strong have governed my life: the longing for love, the search for knowledge, and unbearable pity for the suffering of mankind."

Kota Kimabalu
Malaysia
March 26, 2013
http://andrevltchek.weebly.com

1

The Murderous Legacy of Colonialism

ANDRE VLTCHEK

Between 50 and 55 million people have died around the world as a result of Western colonialism and neo-colonialism since the end of World War II. This relatively short period has arguably seen the greatest number of massacres in human history. Most of them were performed in the name of lofty slogans such as freedom and democracy. A handful of European nations and those governed mainly by citizens of European descent have been advancing Western interests—the interests of the people who "matter"—against those of the great majority of humanity. The slaughter of millions has been accepted and seen as inevitable and even justifiable. And the great majority of the Western public appears to be frighteningly badly informed.

Along with the 55 million or so people killed as the direct result of wars initiated by the West, pro-Western military coups and other conflicts, hundreds of millions have died indirectly, in absolute misery, and silently. Such global arrangements are rarely challenged in the West, and even in the conquered world it is often accepted without any opposition. Has the world gone mad?

NOAM CHOMSKY

Unfortunately there is fierce competition over which is the greatest crime the West has committed. When Columbus landed in the Western hemisphere, there were probably 80–100 million people with advanced civilizations: commerce, cities, etc. Not long afterward about 95 percent of this population had disappeared. In what is now the territory of the United States, there were maybe ten million or so Native Americans, but by 1900, according to the census, there were 200,000 in the country. But all of this is denied. In the leading intellectual, left-liberal journals in the Anglo-American world, it's simply denied ... casually and with no comment.

According to the medical journal *The Lancet*, six million children die every year from lack of elementary medical procedures, which could be provided at virtually no cost. The number is all too familiar. Malnutrition and easily treatable diseases kill 8000 children in Southern Africa alone every day: Rwanda level, but every day. And easily ended.

And we are moving toward what may in fact be the ultimate genocide—the destruction of the environment. And this is barely being addressed; in fact, the United States is going backwards on it. In the U.S. there is now euphoria about the possibility that we may have a hundred years of energy independence as a result of sophisticated techniques of extraction of fossil fuels, that this will preserve American hegemony for another century, that we will become the Saudi Arabia of the world, and so on. President Obama spoke about it enthusiastically in his 2012 State of the Union address. You can read about it in excited articles in the national press, business press and so on. There is some comment on local environmental effects, such as that it destroys the water supplies, wipes out the ecology, etc. But virtually nothing about the question of what the world is going to look like in a hundred years if we proceed with this. That is not discussed. Now these are very fundamental problems. They are kind of intrinsic in the market-oriented societies, where you do not consider what we call externalities. Things that don't enter into any particular transaction, those that affect others: that is not considered.

ANDRE VLTCHEK

I am witnessing the disappearance of several countries in Oceania (the South Pacific). I was based in Samoa for several years and travelled extensively across the region. Several countries, like Tuvalu and Kiribati, but also the Marshall Islands, are already thinking about massive evacuation of their citizens. There are several islands and atolls that are already becoming uninhabitable in Oceania, but also in Maldives and elsewhere. Kiribati may be the first one to disappear as a country. The mass

2   Ebeye Island, Marshall Islands, showing pollution from the nearby U.S. military base at Kwajalein. (Copyright Andre Vltchek)

media says that those countries are sinking. They are actually not sinking at all, but there are tidal waves that go over the atolls and destroy all the vegetation, contaminating water supplies, if there are any. This makes these islands uninhabitable or too dependent on the imports of everything, from water to food.

Surprisingly, when I worked in Tuvalu, there was no foreign press present. There was only one Japanese film crew shooting something irrelevant, some soap opera, on the Funafuti Atoll. It made me think: this was one of the worst affected countries, one that could soon disappear from the face of the earth as sea levels rise, and there was no press coverage whatsoever!

NOAM CHOMSKY

George Orwell had a term for it: "unpeople." The world is divided into people like us, and unpeople—everyone else who do not matter. Orwell was talking about a future totalitarian society, but it applies quite well to us. There is a fine young British diplomatic historian, Mark Curtis, who uses the term unpeople in his study of the post-World War II depredations of the British Empire. We are not concerned with what happens to them.

There are parallels with the treatment of indigenous populations of the so-called Anglosphere, the offshoots of England: the United States, Canada, Australia. These are unusual imperial societies in that they didn't just rule the natives, they eliminated them. They took over their land and settlements and virtually exterminated them in most cases. We don't think about them. We don't ask what happened to them in the past. We deny it in fact.

ANDRE VLTCHEK

Historically this was the case in almost all European colonies, in all parts of the world controlled by European colonial empires.

The first concentration camps were built not by Nazi Germany, but by the British Empire—in Kenya and South Africa. And of course the Holocaust that was performed by Germans on European Jews and Roma was not the first German holocaust; they were involved in terrible massacres in the southern cone of South America and in fact all over the world. Germany had already exterminated the majority of the Herero tribe in Namibia. This is all hardly discussed in Germany and in the rest of Europe. There was no reason for the onslaught, and no logic. The only explanation was absolute spite Germans had for local populations.

But listen to those laments of so many Europeans after World War II—about how that rational and philosophical and essentially peaceful Germany suddenly ran amok, just because it was economically humiliated after World War I! How nobody would expect such an outburst of violence from such nice people. Well, one would not, if one did not consider the Herero people, or Samoans, or Mapuche Indians as human beings, and if one could forget about German colonial history in the rest of Africa.

NOAM CHOMSKY

Even in the case of the Holocaust, the Roma were treated pretty much the way the Jews were. But that's not really mentioned either. Nor is Roma persecution today generally acknowledged. For example, in 2010 the French government decided to expel Roma residents in France to misery and terror in Romania. Can you imagine the French expelling Jewish survivors of the Holocaust to some place where they were still being tortured and terrorised? The country would blow up in fury. This passed without comment!

ANDRE VLTCHEK

Walls were built to separate the Roma in the modern Czech Republic. They were actually building ghettos in the middle of the cities relatively recently, less than a couple of decades ago. This was a very chilling reminder of the 1930s and 40s, when the Czechs collaborated with the Nazis and helped to round-up Roma people. Of course, by the 1990s the Czechs had become staunch allies of the West, and therefore they were an untouchable nation in the eyes of Western mass media. The treatment of Roma in the Czech Republic is much more brutal than anything committed by Mugabe against Zimbabwean white farmers.

But coming back to European colonialism, it feels like colonialism didn't disappear with the end of World War II, or in the 1950s or 60s. The more I travel through the so-called marginal parts of the world, the more it appears that colonialism has solidified itself through much better propaganda and better knowledge of how to deal with the local population. It is actually very scary because in the past there was always an enemy, some tangible villain. It was easy to define the enemy in a colonial army or in the face of some colonial administration. Colonialism continues but it appears that it is much more difficult for local people to point the finger and say exactly what is happening and who their enemies are.

NOAM CHOMSKY

Some of the worst atrocities in the world have been committed over the last few years in the Eastern Congo. Three to five million people may have been killed. And who do you point the finger at? They have been killed by militias, but behind the militias are multinational corporations and governments, and they are not visible.

ANDRE VLTCHEK

Right now I am finishing a long documentary film called *Rwanda Gambit*. It has taken me more than three years to complete it. The numbers we are talking about now are even higher than those you mentioned: six to ten million people killed in DR Congo, which is approximately as many as those killed at the beginning of the twentieth century by the Belgian King Leopold II. And you are right: although it is mostly Rwanda, Uganda, and their proxies who are murdering millions of innocent people, behind this are always Western geopolitical and economic interests.

NOAM CHOMSKY

You don't see the multinational corporations that are using the militias to slaughter people so that they can get access to the coltan that Westerners are using in their cell phones and

3 Street scene in Goma, Democratic Republic of Congo.
(Copyright Andre Vltchek)

other valuable minerals. That's indirect. And there are a lot of atrocities and crimes that you are describing which have that property... but some are quite direct... so take Vietnam, which is the worst crime since World War II. 2011 marked the 50th anniversary of John F. Kennedy's launching of the war. Usually, 50th anniversaries are well commemorated, certainly if they involve monstrosities. But in this case, not a word. In November 1961, Kennedy sent the U.S. Air Force to begin bombing South Vietnam. He authorized napalm, authorized chemical warfare to destroy crops and ground cover, initiated programs which ultimately drove millions of people into so-called "strategic hamlets," in effect concentration camps, or urban slums.

The effects of the chemical warfare are still being felt. If we go to Saigon hospitals—you may have seen them—you can still see those deformed fetuses; the children that were born with all kinds of hideous deformities and abnormalities as a result of all the chemical poisons that literally drenched South Vietnam. But now, several generations down the road, there is no concern.

This also went on in Laos and Cambodia. There is much talk about how terrible Pol Pot's regime in Cambodia was, but there is virtually nothing about what led up to it. In the early 1970s the United States Air Force bombed rural Cambodia to the level of the combined Allied air operations in the Pacific during World War II. They were following Henry Kissinger's instructions regarding a massive bombing campaign against Cambodia: "Anything that flies against anything that moves." I mean that's a call for genocide of the kind that you imply earlier. It will be hard to find anything like it in the archival record. Well, it was mentioned in one sentence in the *New York Times* and then it stopped. The scale of the bombing has never been reported except in scholarly journals, or on the margins. But this is the killing of millions of people, destroying four countries that never recovered. People there know it but don't know what to do about it.

ANDRE VLTCHEK

I lived in Hanoi in Vietnam for several years and I covered the consequences of the Plain of Jars carpet-bombing in Laos by the U.S. Air Force and its allies, which was called the Secret War, but I also wrote plenty about Cambodia. And the conclusions that I arrived at were absolutely shocking: like in the case of so many other places destabilized and ravished by the West, there has been a determined disinformation campaign conducted by Western mass-media outlets. Cambodia during the reign of Pol Pot has been depicted as one of the most dreadful examples of heinous crimes committed by Communism. The true story, the genocide committed against the people of Southeast Asia by the West, had been muted or totally omitted.

The U.S. campaign, using B52s, was to bomb the Laotian and Cambodian countryside to prevent Laos and Cambodia from joining Vietnam in its liberation struggle. Millions were mercilessly murdered. Even today cows are getting their heads blown off, because they chew stones and periodically also bite into the so-called "bombies" which are still all over the place. You can of course also imagine what is still happening to people, to women and children.

Five or six years ago, I worked closely with the Mines Advisory Group (MAG), a large British-based de-mining agency, and they were complaining that several companies who were producing and supplying deadly devices for the war (one of them is now a famous U.S.-based producer of domestic consumer goods) in Indochina are still refusing to share technical data on these weapons, which makes MAG's work much more difficult, because they need to know how to disassemble the mechanism and they need to know how long these devices are going to stay active. This spite, this institutionalized lack of compassion, translates into absolute lack of cooperation that continues to kill hundreds, even thousands, of local people, mainly women and children.

In Cambodia, it all began with the U.S. implanting an illegitimate and corrupt government in the capital, Phnom Penh. When we talk about the atrocities of Khmer Rouge, of so-called Communism, I find it quite questionable, almost grotesque. Uneducated and cut-off from the rest of the world, most of Cambodia had no clue about Communist ideology after Pol Pot returned from France, where he managed to get radicalized at local cafés. What I was told on the ground in Cambodia was that, during the Khmer Rouge era, the atrocities were largely down to the people of the countryside settling scores with the urban elites of Phnom Penh.

Phnom Penh was actually fully collaborating with the U.S. during the bombing campaigns and the people in the countryside developed a profound hatred for the city dwellers, whom they saw as collaborators and often at the root of their suffering. It all had hardly anything to do with the Communist ideology. And there is no doubt that more people were murdered during the U.S. bombing campaigns of the Cambodian countryside than by Khmer Rouge actions.

Then, when it all was over and Vietnam liberated Cambodia and kicked out the Khmer Rouge from power, the U.S. ambassador to the UN was "demanding return of the legitimate government," meaning the Khmer Rouge. The U.S. was fighting the war against Vietnam, a Soviet ally, not against some self-proclaimed and freakish Maoist regime.

But the disinformation campaign of the West is clear: to indict Communist ideology, to connect it to Pol Pot's atrocities. In one of my reports from Cambodia I argued that were Pol Pot and his clique to encourage villagers to kill city dwellers under the banner of some South American football club or jogging shoes, the outcome would be the same.

NOAM CHOMSKY

Scholars have pointed out that in the entire history of Cambodia the part that is by far the most extensively investigated is the three years of Khmer Rouge rule. More is known about Cambodia in that period than the rest of the entire history of the country. But just take the few years before, virtually nothing is known about that time. What we do know is that the Khmer Rouge was a pretty marginal group in 1970 but mobilized a huge army of enraged peasants, who of course went right after the urban elites, whom they saw as the perpetrators.

They didn't see the hand of Washington behind the urban elites. It's a little bit like Eastern Congo and coltan—you don't see who's killing you. I think that is very striking in the West as well. Just one example, serious even though remote in scale: in Wisconsin, the Republican governor eliminated collective bargaining for unions. There were huge protests, and a new election for the governorship, a recall vote, was demanded. But the Republican actually won in the recall. It is interesting to see why. There was a very effective propaganda campaign that convinced suffering people that the source of their woes is their neighbors. Not the banks that are the actual perpetrators in the crimes that destroyed the economy—they are too remote. What you can see is your neighbors who are a little better off than you are. Your neighbor might be, say, a firefighter who has a pension, and you don't have a pension, so you turn your anger against him. Not against the people who crushed the economy, because they are somewhere else; they are often in skyscrapers in New York. There was an immense propaganda campaign with a huge amount of money behind it. The Nazis did it with the Jews: "They are the ones who are responsible for your hunger and the depression."

ANDRE VLTCHEK

Yes, there could be a very powerful parallel drawn between what happened in Southeast Asia and what is taking place in Rwanda, Uganda, and the Democratic Republic of Congo. We see militias doing the killing and millions dying. The local people are often described as barbarians, almost animals. The Western governments and corporations are too far away and hardly held responsible.

The knowledge in Europe and the U.S. regarding these occurrences is minimal. And Europe is the continent that prides itself for being educated and informed. Most Africans know, but Europeans whose companies are involved know close to nothing. Or they choose to know nothing.

Everything is interconnected. Robert Mugabe became "evil" in the West around the time he participated in stopping the second attempt to overthrow the government of DR Congo by Rwandan forces; in reality Western proxies. Sarcastic tongues in East Africa talk about South Sudan being a reward given to Ugandan President Yoweri Museveni for his "good work" in the region, on the West's behalf.

In Congo we are talking about unimaginable suffering, a super-genocide, something that could now easily compete with what was done to the Congo by Leopold II a century ago.

I have to repeat the numbers once again, as they are dreadful, unimaginable. When I was filming in Washington last year and one of the presidential candidates in DR Congo, Ben Kalala, told me that we are talking about six to eight million people. Some say ten million. He said: "Look, in Rwanda about 800 thousand people died. I feel for them because they are human beings, but the whole world is talking about the 1994 genocide. In Congo we have six to eight million people who have been killed."

This is just in the last few years, which again resembles quite clearly the rule of Leopold II, when about ten million also died. If you didn't perform well on the rubber plantations your hands would be cut off, and people were burnt alive in their huts. It was a great warning to the world of what can be done both by Western constitutional monarchies and multi-party "democracies." Of course this was not done in Antwerp or Bruges, but in the "heart of darkness," far away from inquisitive eyes. So Belgians killed more people in Africa than what was then the population of their own country.

NOAM CHOMSKY

I once out of curiosity looked up the most famous edition of the *Encyclopedia Britannica*. It was 1910 or so, and I looked up King Leopold II. There was an entry of course, where it talked about the wonderful things he did, how he built up the country and so on. At the end it said something like "he sometimes treated his people harshly"—yes, such as murdering ten million people.

ANDRE VLTCHEK

When I was in Brussels in 2011, I stumbled on so many statues of Leopold II. He is still honored immensely in Belgium, so although we know that what he did to the population in Congo was genocidal even by European colonialist standards, he is still considered one of the national heroes of Belgium.

At some point the Belgian state actually took away his private colonies, and they "nationalized" them. This sounds like a joke, of course. Instead of letting go of the colonies, after realizing that ten million people were murdered, the Belgian state took them away from the perverse monarch and began to run them by itself. And I am sure that they convinced, re-educated, many Congolese people into believing that there was nothing wrong with being colonized.

NOAM CHOMSKY

It's kind of an interesting fact that colonized people often accept and even honor their own repression. Once in Kolkata, I went to visit the Victoria Memorial Museum, and when you get there, the first thing that greets you is a big statue of Sir Robert Clive, one of the people who destroyed India. I was taken by the guides through hall after hall of hideously ugly paintings, of the British beating Indians and humiliating them and so on. Then I went to Queen Victoria's tearoom, which had somehow been reconstituted, and it's truly like some national shrine. All this was the symbol of India's destruction, and who knows how many people were killed.

ANDRE VLTCHEK

I visited that place on several occasions. It is both grotesque and telling. I never saw a museum in India being so well

4   Statue of British imperialist Robert Clive at
the Victoria Memorial Hall in Kolkata, India.
(Copyright Andre Vltchek)

attended as the Victoria Memorial Museum. Thousands of
people are regularly pouring into it, every day. And it is lovingly
maintained. The British Empire certainly indoctrinated millions
of its subjects. For instance, in Malaysia elites are still doing all
they can to appear even more British than people from the UK.
All monuments from the days of the Empire are painstakingly
preserved. Even in Sabah, in Borneo, they have English tearooms
and restored mansions turned museums that used to belong

to the colonizers. And the ultimate aim of young educated Malaysian people is to study at some prestigious university in England; to basically shed their Malayness and become as close to the former colonialists as possible. The same trend could be seen in Kenya, where the local elites, those that are now plundering their own country on behalf of the neo-colonial masters, are dressing like the English gentlemen used to, some decades ago. Kenyan judges are wearing wigs identical to those worn by their counterparts in Britain, and many of those with high standing are imitating an English accent.

In Southeast Asia, many people are convinced that the colonial rulers governed them justly. There is an absolutely pathetic discussion going on now in Indonesia, Malaysia, and Singapore on why Malaysia is so much ahead of Indonesia, for example. Many of them think that this is because of the wonderful rule of the British Empire in Malaya; so many Indonesians are actually complaining that the Dutch were not as good colonial rulers as the Brits!

You could see the same, until very recently, even in Peru. Lima used to be the capital of the Viceroy of Spain and one of the centers of the crimes against humanity committed by the West. There used to be, on the Plaza del Armas in front of the Presidential Palace, an enormous statue of Francisco Pizarro. It was there until a few years ago. Now of course they have a new government; they moved the statue down to the park. It's still there, just not on Plaza del Armas. But they would not destroy it, even now under the relatively socialist or left-leaning system. All of Latin America is dotted with symbols of the conquest. It is as if a certain sector of society feels some nostalgia for the colonial whip.

NOAM CHOMSKY

There is a little bit of reaction now. For example, in 1992 in the Dominican Republic the government was going to have a huge celebration of Columbus's arrival and they erected some large monuments, but I think they were all demolished by popular forces.

There can be an intellectual and moral colonization as well as political and economic colonization. It has deep roots and there are many other examples of it. Take, say, the status of women. For millennia women accepted that the natural order was for them to be the property of their fathers and husbands: in the United States it is only in the last several decades that this has been seriously challenged. For example, until 1975 women didn't have a guaranteed legal right to serve in the juries in federal trials. If you had asked my grandmother, let's say, whether she was oppressed, she would not have even understood the word! That was the role of women, to serve others, and it was internalized. The main achievement of hierarchy and oppression is to get the un-people to accept that it's natural.

Is there any consciousness of colonial history among Europeans?

ANDRE VLTCHEK

No, grotesquely there is very little consciousness. I see it even among my Spanish friends, and I am talking about people who actually work or used to work for the United Nations and other prestigious international organizations—quite an educated crowd. There is a naïve, ignorance about their history. I clash even with my relatively progressive friends from the media and publishing in France over French colonialism.

That's how far it gets. Unrelenting admiration for General de Gaulle, even by the center-left and their belief that France was never truly as bad a colonizer as were the others. As if Africa or Indochina or the Caribbean never existed. You know, in some places the French managed to massacre the entire native population, such as on the island of Grenada. Those they did not kill were jumping from the cliffs to escape the horror of falling into their hands. And on Easter Island, which is now Chilean territory in Polynesia, they came extremely close to that 100 percent "success ratio."

I also think that Dutch perception about colonialism in Indonesia is absolutely primitive, appalling, sick. I met somebody sitting in a Phnom Penh bar, holding his head after visiting Jakarta and repeating in drunken stupor: "We should have never left." And the man I am referring to was an EU official!

And there is hardly any German perception regarding their colonialism in Africa. I heard nobody discussing Namibia in Stuttgart or Munich, except as a nice vacation spot with spectacular dunes.

In Chile, right-wingers say that Pinochet did some very good things and very bad things. And that's the same thing you hear in the UK about colonialism. Of course there would never be any deep remorse, grief, or perception of guilt regarding what had happened during the partition of Pakistan and India. This was to a large extent set up by the British Empire and probably led to the worst round of massacres in modern history, with the only serious competition coming from the Western-backed 1965 coup in Indonesia and the present-day genocide in the Democratic Republic of Congo. And there is hardly any understanding of what has been done to Africa and the Middle East.

NOAM CHOMSKY

A group of expatriate Algerian physicists—one of whom was here at MIT, so I got to know him—put together a very detailed study of the atrocities in Algeria in the 1990s. Their view was that many of the atrocities that were attributed to the Islamists were actually carried out by the government with fake Islamist costumes and so on. They went through details of case after case. A standard massacre might be a big massacre in a poor neighborhood, a couple of kilometers away from a large military base, that would go on for three days and nobody would intervene, and then after everybody was killed or kicked out a general would enter the neighborhood and enrich himself. Case after case like that . . . they thought it was being orchestrated by French intelligence and they asked me to write an introduction. I looked into it and I got as much evidence as I could. It was pretty persuasive so I did write the introduction, quite toned down but implications remained.

The book was finally published. They couldn't get a French publisher, so it had to be published in Switzerland. They tried to have a press conference in Paris when it was released but no French journalist would show up. And so the book ended up unknown in France. I told a friend of mine who was working in the American Library in Paris about the book. He got a copy and put it in the Library. He told me that it was the only copy in France. And this is about a recent current event, about atrocities in Algeria in the 1990s in which France likely had a hand.

ANDRE VLTCHEK

I think this is very revealing. The problem is also that intellectuals in the United States think that people in Europe

19

are better informed than those outside it, that they have a much wider sense of what can be discussed. I found out that this is maybe only the case in regard to issues that are directly related to the United States. Otherwise there is a screaming ignorance in Europe. In general, I find educated people in Asia, Latin America, and Africa better informed on current affairs than their European counterparts. I find Westerners in general, and Europeans in particular, extremely indoctrinated and obsessed with perceptions of their own uniqueness. Many see themselves as chosen people, after going through a one-sided education and after relying on their media outlets, without studying alternative sources.

And to go back, when you asked me what is the situation in Europe and how much they know about colonialism, I think they know next to nothing. I think that the lack of knowledge and lack of interest on the topic is extremely shameful and revealing. Europeans make sure that they remain ignorant of their horrid crimes, about the genocides they committed and are still involved in. What do they know about what their governments and companies were and are doing in DR Congo? They know nothing, simply because they choose to know nothing. It is much safer to complain about mismanaged foreign aid by corrupt governments in poor countries!

NOAM CHOMSKY

When you do talk about it, what are their reactions?

ANDRE VLTCHEK

They are very often defensive. I find this in France, in Germany, in Spain, and in the UK, although the UK has a bigger critical

5   Column from which the Portuguese used to
hang African slaves preserved in the center of
town, Cape Verde. (Copyright Andre Vltchek)

mass than any other European country, perhaps because it is
becoming a truly multicultural society. The ignorance in Europe
is not only towards its colonialist history, but also even in regard
to the history of the European continent.

NOAM CHOMSKY

I found some very interesting experiences in Spain. I was giving
talks in Barcelona in 1990, about 15 years after Franco went.

I made some references to famous events that took place in Barcelona in 1936–7. Younger people had no sense of the civil war. It was only people of my age who understood what I was referring to. And then I happened to go to Oviedo right after that and give some talks there. In Oviedo in 1934 there had been a left uprising and then the troops came in and destroyed it. The Town Hall was occupied, people were murdered and so on. So I was talking in the Town Hall, thinking they knew the history of the place, but there was no reaction. The only people who knew what I was talking about were people of my age. The rest, nothing!

ANDRE VLTCHEK

Yes. It is illustrative of how the Spanish engage with the entire Franco period. In South America—Chile, Argentina, Uruguay—they are much more open about the past; people there are brave.

NOAM CHOMSKY

You are right. I was in Mexico with my daughter who used to live in Nicaragua. I was reading *La Jornada* which I think is quite a good newspaper and they had a report on a national biographical dictionary that had just come out in Spain, published by the Spanish Academy, a prestigious publication, and there is an entry on Franco of course and he was described as a conservative nationalist who was quite good for the country. Negrin in contrast was a criminal.

2

Concealing the Crimes of the West

ANDRE VLTCHEK

I have statisticians working with me, trying to establish the number of people who vanished after World War II as a result of colonialism and neo-colonialism. As I said at the start of our discussion, it looks to be between 50 and 55 million. However, the exact number is probably irrelevant, whether it is 40 million or 60 million. The magnitude is so tremendous, although somehow Western culture manages to get away with these crimes, and still keeps the world convinced that it has a sort of moral mandate; that it has the right to dictate to the world through its organizations and its media, its own values. How are they achieving this?

NOAM CHOMSKY

A book came out in France in 1997 called *The Black Book of Communism*. It was quickly translated to English, to glorifying reviews everywhere. It claimed that there were 100 million victims of Communism, and how could people be so evil, that it is unimaginable etc., etc. Well, let's put aside the question of the validity of their analysis; let's say it is right. The main charges are against China, in particular because of the great famine, where they estimated maybe 25 to 30 million people died, and there was just total horror in the discussion of this. Around the same time a number of academic studies came out by very well-known people such as Amartya Sen, a Nobel Laureate in Economics and a specialist in famines. Sen, with an economist in India, made an interesting comparative study. They compared India and China from liberation in the late 1940s to 1979. They stopped at 1979 because that's when the so-called capitalist reforms were initiated in China. So they limited their comparison to the Maoist period. What they found is that 100 million people died in democratic capitalist India, as compared with China during this period, simply by India's failure to institute health reforms, education reforms or rural aid programs and so on. In fact the way they put it was that every eight years India killed as many people as China killed during its years of shame, the great famine. And they point out that both of these are political crimes, they have to do with the nature of the socio-economic system and the political system that was instituted. Well, that's one country, India, 100 million deaths. If Sen did the same analysis worldwide under what's called democratic capitalism, the figures would be phenomenal.

I remember when Amartya Sen won his Nobel Prize, I was interviewed by a lot of people and I kept pointing this out. I found one journalist who was willing to mention it; an Indian journalist. But the crimes of Communism, I mean, we not only lament, we can't even imagine the hideousness of them. How can humans sink to this level, yet we can't even see what's there before our eyes? The only thing that anyone can see, let alone mention, is the Chinese famine. That takes a remarkable kind of selective blindness on the part of the people we live with. The faculty club, the editorial boards and so on, they just can't see it. It's just as when the *New York Review of Books*, the leading kind of left-liberal intellectual journal, blandly publishes an article saying that when Columbus reached the Western hemisphere there were maybe a million people, hunter-gatherers struggling around and so on... Off by many tens of millions. They didn't just vanish, you know... but not a comment....

ANDRE VLTCHEK

There is very interesting research being done now by Geoffrey C. Gunn, one of my friends from the University of Nagasaki in Japan. He is actually writing an entire book on the Chinese famine and on the impact of Japanese colonial or imperial policy. Not that they, the Japanese, triggered the famine on purpose, but because they were moving resources and changing the structure of Chinese food distribution at the end of the war. He is arguing in his book that it had nothing to do with the Communist ideology but with the imperialism of the Japanese.

NOAM CHOMSKY

There are books in Japan now denying the Nanking Massacre. And actually the U.S. have helped with the amnesia. At the end of World War II, the U.S. ruled most of Asia and Japan. They occupied Japan, and could basically run Asia, and they did have a peace treaty, the San Francisco Peace Treaty, in which the U.S. insisted that the Japanese crimes be limited to those from December 7, 1941; nothing that happened in the preceding ten years could be discussed. As a result, independent Asian countries just refused to come, other than the Philippines, but that was virtually a colony, and maybe Ceylon, which was still under British occupation. But India wouldn't come; Indonesia would not come, because the U.S. was wiping out the major Japanese crimes. The U.S. wasn't affected by them so as far as we were concerned, they didn't happen. They just affected un-people.

ANDRE VLTCHEK

And we have the same situation now in Rwanda. The same structure of the Arusha-based Tribunal (ICTR), the same principle, that there is a time limitation for the crimes that can be addressed, while the side we support—the RPF and Paul Kagame—are excluded from the process.

NOAM CHOMSKY

If we look at the international tribunals, the only people who are indicted are overwhelmingly Africans and one or two people who are enemies of the West, like Milosevic. And the Africans are also always from the side that we don't like. But have there not been any other crimes committed in the last few years?

Take the invasion of Iraq—nothing can be potentially regarded as criminal. Forget about Nuremberg and the rest of modern international law. In fact there is a legal reason for that, which is not too well known. The United States is self-immunized from any prosecution. When they joined the World Court in 1946, the U.S. basically initiated the modern International Court of Justice, which it joined but with the reservation that the U.S. cannot be tried on any international treaty—meaning the UN charter, the charter of the Organization of the American States, the Geneva Conventions. The U.S. is self-immunized from any trial on those issues. And the Court has accepted that. So for example when Nicaragua brought a case against the United States at the World Court for the terrorist attacks against

Nicaragua, most of the case was thrown out because it invoked the charter of the Organization of American States, which bars interventions strongly, and the U.S. is not subject to that and the Court accepted it.

In fact the same happened, interestingly, at the trial where Yugoslavia brought a case against NATO for the bombing to the International Court of Justice, I think, and the United States excluded itself from the case and the Tribunal agreed because one of the charges mentioned was that it was a genocide, and when the United States signed the Genocide Convention after 40 years, it had a reservation saying it was "inapplicable to the United States," and so therefore the Court rightly excused the United States from prosecution. There are literally legal barriers established just in case anyone dares to try to bring some charge against the powerful. I am sure you recall when the Rome Treaty was signed, and the International Criminal Court was established, the U.S. refused to participate . . . but then it was more than that. Congress passed legislation, which the Bush administration happily signed, which granted the White House authority to invade The Hague by force in case any American was brought there. In Europe it is sometimes called the Netherlands Invasion Act. Well, that was passed here enthusiastically, so the self-immunization is at many levels. One is the impossibility to perceive, such as when you deny what happened to the indigenous population in the United States, when you just can't see it even if it is in front of your eyes. The other is that it's actually fortified by legislation.

ANDRE VLTCHEK

Look at the attacks against China. Whenever China makes an error, the smallest error, like the mining disasters in Zambia in which its companies were involved and several people died – several, not millions – it becomes the target of negative propaganda by the local and international press. Then the tragedy of several people who might have died in some mining accident gets suddenly elevated to the same level of the tragedy of hundreds of millions of those who have been slaughtered by the Western colonial and neo-colonial powers.

NOAM CHOMSKY

There have been very sophisticated propaganda systems developed in the last hundred years and they colonized minds including the minds of the perpetrators. That's why the intellectual classes in the West generally can't see it. One interesting example of this, which struck me over the years, has to do with Eastern Europe and Eastern European dissidents. Eastern European dissidents like Václav Havel are very famous in the West and greatly honored… and they suffered undoubtedly and many were put in jail. On the other hand they must be the most privileged dissidents in the world. They had the entire Western propaganda system worshipping them. No dissidents anywhere else had anything like that. There were some very striking cases right after the fall of the Berlin Wall, such as what happened in San Salvador immediately afterward: six leading Latin American intellectuals, Jesuit priests, were brutally murdered in the Jesuit university by the Atlacatl Battalion, an elite unit of the Salvadoran army, which had already killed I don't know how many thousands of people.

They had just returned from renewed training at the John F. Kennedy Special Warfare School in North Carolina. They came back and on the explicit orders of the high command, which is in close contact with the American Embassy, they were sent into the university to murder these priests and anyone else who was around—so they murdered the housekeeper, the daughter, so there would not be any witnesses. Right after that, Václav Havel came to the United States and he spoke before a Joint Session of Congress where he got just rapturous applause, especially when he described the United States as the defenders of freedom. That was his words, "the defenders of freedom," who have just brutally murdered half a dozen of his counterparts in a place which is inhabited by un-people. No comment. Anyone who mentioned the remarkable and illuminating event was denounced.

It is just inconceivable that it could have been reversed. If Havel and half a dozen of his associates had been viciously murdered by security forces trained and armed by the Russians, and then Father Ellacuria, one of the murdered Jesuit priests, had gone to Russia and spoken to the joint session of the Duma and praised them as the defenders of freedom . . . the world would have blown up. But in this case it is invisible, no matter how many times it is brought up, and if it is even noticed it just sets off a stream of hysteria.

I think that accounts for a pretty striking difference between the behavior of East European intellectuals and Latin American ones. East Europeans typically are concerned with themselves; they say "we suffered." Latin Americans are far more humanistic and internationalist. It's inconceivable that Father Ellacuria could have done what Havel did. I think it comes from the fact that while they were very harshly treated, they were also coddled and worshipped. It was a badge of honor for Westerners to go to Eastern Europe to visit them; I tried to do it too, but I wasn't permitted entry, because they wouldn't accept my visa application. On the other hand, those who went to Central America while we were murdering intellectuals and innumerable others there were certainly not considered so noble. Rather, mocked as "sandalistas" and in other ways.

There's much more. For instance, there is a community of Mayan refugees from Guatemala a few miles from here [Cambridge, Massachusetts]. To this day they are fleeing from the wreckage left by the virtual genocide in the highlands 30 years ago under Reagan. The general who was in charge is now actually being tried, but no mention of Reagan, who praised him as a man totally dedicated to democracy but getting a bum rap from the human rights groups who were run by "leftists." There is a good deal of anger about illegal immigration, but why are these people fleeing? Well, we can't look at that because there is too much blood on our hands, so it is forgotten about—Laos, Cambodia, you can pick a thousand cases like this.

3

Propaganda and the Media

ANDRE VLTCHEK

When I speak in China, I am not censored. This is actually rather surprising because I keep arguing that they should follow the Latin American example and go back to Communism without the Cultural Revolution baggage. And they publish this. I was on CCTV—their National TV—and for half an hour I was talking about very sensitive issues. And I felt much freer in Beijing than when the BBC interviews me, because the BBC doesn't even let me speak, without demanding a full account of what exactly I am intending to say.

NOAM CHOMSKY

I had interviews with their television and my friends in China told me that they were translated accurately; they didn't cut things out, even when they were pretty critical. I actually had the same experience with Iran. I have been on Press TV a couple of times. In speaking about Iran I had been careful about being critical about the regime, and that's in English so I can hear it. I picked it up later and they ran it straight.

ANDRE VLTCHEK

I had the same experience when the *Iran Times* interviewed me recently—they did not censor anything. What is really happening, Noam, is that people in the West are so used to thinking that we are so democratic in terms of the way our media is run and covers the stories. Even if we know it's not the case, we still, subconsciously, expect that it's still somehow better than in other places and it is actually shocking when we realize that a place like China or Turkey or Iran would run more unedited or uncensored pieces than our own mainstream media outlets. Let me put it this way: Chinese television and newspapers are much more critical of their economic and political system than our television stations or newspapers are of ours. Imagine ABC, CBS, or NBC coming on air and beginning to question the basics of capitalism or the Western parliamentary system.

NOAM CHOMSKY

There are other ways to censor things here, too. Our media here have techniques, which aren't exactly censorship, but prevent anything from being said. There is a word I learned from the news director for Ted Koppel, the anchor for *Nightline*, one of ABC's big news programs. He was once asked in an interview why I am never on. And he had a good answer. He said that one reason is because Chomsky sounds like he's from Neptune, nobody can understand anything he says. And then he said the other reason is that he lacks concision. What? I had never heard the word before but it is an interesting word. What it means is: you have to talk in some way that can be fitted in between two commercials. So you can say three sentences. If you want to say in three sentences that China is a totalitarian state you can say it, you know. If you want to say something like the U.S. is the biggest terrorist state in the world, they are not going to stop you, but you do sound like you are from Neptune, because you are not given the next five minutes to explain it.

So you have two choices, to either repeat propaganda, repeat standard doctrine, or sound like you are a lunatic. That's about the only thing you can do. So of course it comes out all very bland. I don't think there is a program on a commercial channel where people can discuss something for a half an hour.

ANDRE VLTCHEK

No, and if there is, there are the commercials which reduce that half an hour to just 20 minutes, if that. Recently I was invited on to the BBC program *World Have Your Say*, and it was about China again and it had this absolutely ridiculous and disrespectful title, it was "Should China Be Respected?" And they invited ten panelists to discuss whether the country with the largest population and one of the oldest cultures should be respected or not, and they didn't even find it ridiculous themselves.

NOAM CHOMSKY

And you had five minutes or two minutes?

ANDRE VLTCHEK

I didn't even have that. They invited some people from the U.S. State Department, and some academics, and then it was supposed to be me and some intellectual from Africa who happened to be very pro-Chinese. Before they let me speak, and it was actually a couple of weeks after I was on CCTV, where I was given free hand, the BBC invited me to listen, and then there was this long silence. I had to sit in front of my computer,

I was online, I had earphones on, in Jakarta, and I was waiting endlessly for them to invite me to speak.

Finally they connected me, so I could hear all this anti-China propaganda nonsense for three or four minutes. I could not speak; it was just one-way; I could only listen. And then I heard this little voice from far away London: Mr. Vltchek, are you ready to go? I said "Yes, I am." "What are you going to say"? I was asked. I said, "Well, you know, I am going to say it on the air in a few seconds... You will hear it, madam." "Oh no, no," she protested gently. "Would you be so kind and tell us?" To make a long story short, I was not allowed to go on the air.

Eventually I told them what I wanted to say, that what they—the BBC—are doing is disrespectful and patronizing and that it reminds millions of people all over the world of the British colonial past and their attitude towards the "locals" and lesser people. I told her that it is the equivalent of somebody asking whether the UK should be respected or not, where the consequent discussion focuses purely on how the UK has murdered people in Afghanistan and Iraq. And even that would be much more objective than the discussion the BBC was conducting about China. They thanked me, and never let me participate in the discussion. Later, one of their producers wrote me an apologetic email.

NOAM CHOMSKY

They didn't let you speak?

ANDRE VLTCHEK

No, and I was there, officially invited to participate in the discussion by one of the BBC producers. What actually impressed me about all this was that they probably have an entire army of such people, trained in screening the guests they are going to interview. Their censors, or their "screening personnel" have to be very quick and very good at what they are doing. Just one person cannot do it. Probably many, if not most, of the people get screened like that, except those from the political or business establishment. Of course in a country like Czechoslovakia, when the system collapsed, people doing this kind of job would be called many different names. But in the West it is all considered quite normal and legitimate.

NOAM CHOMSKY

Actually, I was once invited onto *Nightline* around the time of the fall of the Berlin wall. They called me up and said: "Would you want to come on?" I said: "For how long?" They said: "A few minutes." I figured this is just going to be a set up. So I said: "I am sorry, I can't make it." A couple of minutes later I got a phone call from my friend Alex Cockburn and he said that he has just been called by *Nightline*, and he asked me whether I thought he should do it? And I told him: "I don't think you should; they are just setting you up." But he decided he would do it anyway.

So I turned on the program to watch. What happened was something like this. The program started by showing large crowds celebrating the Berlin Wall falling, you know, huge excitement... and then they turned to Cockburn, who was sitting in some studio somewhere and said: "Well, Mr. Cockburn what do you have to say about this?" You know, implying "how are you going to handle this?" And he got about two sentences in and then they said: "Thank you Mr. Cockburn!" Then they went back to the celebration, now that they had got this "Communist sympathizer" out of the way, and shown him off as somebody who's refusing to celebrate. It was very carefully constructed.

ANDRE VLTCHEK

It is actually very interesting how bulletproof the system is because usually the "comrades" in Eastern Europe would make many mistakes along the way, make fools out of themselves... while the system here is very solid.

NOAM CHOMSKY

It is very sophisticated, yes. Lenin and the Leninists tried to model themselves in the early days on American commercial advertising. But it was so clumsy that it just didn't work. On the other hand, when the Nazis did it, it worked very effectively.

ANDRE VLTCHEK

In a way the German Nazis were building their system in interaction with the U.S. The Nazis were part of the West. And many European and U.S. concepts inspired them, particularly those related to colonialism and mass production, but also advertisement, as you mentioned, as advertising is a very effective form of propaganda.

NOAM CHOMSKY

They were part of the same general Western culture. And then, as you say, in the end people couldn't listen to Russian propaganda. They wouldn't believe it.

ANDRE VLTCHEK

It is incredible how bad the Soviet propaganda was and how bad Chinese propaganda has been. That's why, despite their tremendous achievements in the past decades, the Chinese are losing the ideological war with the West. They cannot compete with Western propaganda. I don't want to go so far as to say that Tiananmen Square was one of the by-products of this situation, but what is clear is that what the world thinks is what has been hammered home to its subconscious by Western propaganda for years, decades, centuries. And the Communist or Chinese official propaganda are so weak that they can't even defend their own countries, let alone influence Western countries to change their political, social, and imperialist system; something that is long overdue.

The Soviets never managed to hammer into the public's subconscious that they were the ones who facilitated the liberation of dozens of countries all over the world, and that they were basically supporting all major resistance against imperialism and colonialism on all continents. Not to speak about the fact that they were the ones who carried the greatest burden in defeating Nazism and therefore saving the planet.

But it is Western propaganda that is capable of mobilizing the masses for whatever ends or goals anywhere in the world. For whatever reasons, it can trigger coups, conflicts, terrible violence, and "strive for change." It can call the most peaceful large country on earth the most violent; it can describe it as the real threat to world peace; and it can call a bunch of Western nations that have been, for centuries, terrorizing the world, the true upholders of peace and democracy, and almost everybody believes it. Almost all people in the West believe it. Most of the people on this planet do... because Western propaganda is so perfect, so advanced. And China, Venezuela, Russia, Iran, Bolivia, Cuba, Zimbabwe, and Eritrea are not the only victims of this, naturally. Any country that stands in the way of Western interests becomes legitimate target.

NOAM CHOMSKY

I spent a week in Laos in 1970. It was the first time I had ever had real experience with journalists in the field. Usually hardly any Western journalists would be in Laos, but Nixon had just made a big speech about how North Vietnamese tanks were converging on Vientiane. So a ton of journalists flew in; all the big shots, including top people from CBS, the *New York Times*, the BBC. There were only two hotels for them to stay in, and most of the time they spent in the bar.

As soon as I got off the plane, I was met by an International Voluntary Services worker who was really involved with Laos. He knew Laos; he was living in a village, he was the one who exposed the story of the bombings in the Plain of Jars, so he grabbed me as soon as I came off the plane. He had been trying for years to try to get people to pay attention to this. I spent pretty much the whole week going around with him. We went out to refugee camps. It was right after the CIA had driven about 30,000 people out of the Plain of Jars and they were in refugee camps around Vientiane. This was the first time you could get direct stories of what was going on up there. They had been living in caves for two years; there were horrible stories. Few of the journalists would go out there.

ANDRE VLTCHEK

The U.S. was penetrating the caves with missiles, killing hundreds, sometimes thousands, of civilians who were hiding there. Some caves are in fact enormous mass graves. I spoke to several people who managed to survive there...

NOAM CHOMSKY

Yes, the missiles came and those who survived—they described it. You know, at least some survived in the caves. They told the stories that finally, after years, emerged. So I spent a lot of time in the camps. In Vientiane, I met underground Pathet Lao cadres, people in the government who were actually sympathetic to the Pathet Lao and the Lao people, many interesting things. But I also went to the American Embassy. The story that the journalists were reporting was that there were 50,000 North Vietnamese troops in Laos and that's why the U.S. was bombing the Ho Chi Minh Trail, while actually they were bombing the Plain of Jars. And so I was curious—where did this story come from? I couldn't get any of the journalists there to explain.

They didn't know, they just repeated it. What they were told at the 5 o'clock briefings was what they put into their reports. So I went to the Embassy and I asked if I could see the "political officer," meaning the CIA agent. So the guy came down; he was very friendly. He asked what I wanted. I said I was interested in looking into the background of these reports. He said, "oh, great." He took me up to a room, brought in a ton of documents; he said "you can't copy them but you can take notes if you like." And I went on doing that—he told me I was the first person who had ever asked.

It turned out that there was a report that maybe one battalion of 2,500 North Vietnamese troops was up somewhere in the North where the U.S. had a radar station, the one that was being used to bomb North Vietnam. That was the whole story. And hardly a single journalist would visit the refugee camps. There was one stringer for the *Far Eastern Economic Review*, he came along, but almost none of those other guys who flew in for the big show wanted to go; they didn't care.

6   Monument to the American War in Hanoi, Vietnam.
(Copyright Andre Vltchek)

Every morning a group of tall blond American men came down to breakfast in the hotel at 6 a.m. and sat in the corner somewhere, disappeared, and came back at around 5 o'clock and had a drink or did whatever they wanted to do. Everyone could guess that they were Air America pilots, the CIA cover, probably off to bomb the Plain of Jars, but nobody asked the questions. And in fact, this whole business about the supposed North Vietnamese tanks—when they were having drinks at the bar, they were always laughing about it. But they published it, anyway. It was the most amazing insight into how foreign correspondents reporting sometimes works.

There were one or two exceptions; there were a couple of people who did some things on their own, very good people who were doing hard, serious work. But largely they just didn't want to know. They wanted to repeat what was given to them at the 5 o'clock briefing and then have a drink... and enjoy Vientiane... but it was shocking. I don't know if it is worse now.

ANDRE VLTCHEK

Now there is almost no independent reporting, except in the electronic media and just a few print publications that are absolutely broke, most of them can't even pay their writers.

NOAM CHOMSKY

Once I happened to be in Islamabad, just when the U.S. was invading Afghanistan, and Islamabad was the one place where journalists could get to near the fighting. So tons of journalists were there, they were all trying to report on Afghanistan and it was the same story: sitting around the bar in the hotel, having fun. There was a time when an American missile destroyed the Al Jazeera facilities in Kabul and they said, "well, it was a mistake." Every journalist there was just laughing about it. They all took it for granted that they were trying to destroy it, but not one would report it. They just reported the same line. That was Afghanistan but I have seen the same in the West Bank and Central America... Many reporters wouldn't go into the field, with some honorable and courageous exceptions.

ANDRE VLTCHEK

Everywhere the same. I saw it of course in Indonesia; I saw it in India during the Gujarat massacres, and in Sri Lanka. I covered many, many conflicts and of course what I noticed is that there is a tremendous discipline in covering the events that are either supposed not to be covered or supposed to be covered in a certain way. So at the beginning when I was getting into serious journalism and working for all kind of mass media outlets, like ABC News and Asahi Shimbun in Japan, I thought that maybe at least sometimes I would be allowed to cover stories properly. I was in East Timor during the mid-1990s for ABC News; the one in the U.S., not in Australia. I tried to cover the Ermera massacre. I was arrested. Most of my films were confiscated. I was tortured. I was released, eventually. But ABC was not interested and wouldn't run anything. I said, "look we could get back there, somehow, I know how to smuggle an entire crew into Dili." But there was no appetite, no interest, no follow up.

NOAM CHOMSKY

I had a good friend, Charlie Glass, who was the Middle East correspondent for ABC TV for years. He was a very good person, but a kind of maverick. He didn't go along with them and they finally pretty much threw him out. In 1986, the evening of the bombing of Libya, he called me from Tripoli, around 6:30 at night and he said you should watch the 7 o'clock news tonight. In those days all three channels had their major news programs at 7 and he knew I never watch television but he said "watch it tonight." He couldn't tell me why. I turned on the television set at 7 o'clock. Precisely at 7 o'clock, the bombing started. All the studios were there.

ANDRE VLTCHEK

They knew in advance.

NOAM CHOMSKY

Exactly. All the major channels. And it was no small logistical feat. It was a six-hour flight from London, because France didn't let them cross their territory, and so they had to go over the Atlantic. They timed the bombing for prime-time television. So what happened was you watched all these exciting things going off, and then it switches over to the Pentagon, you get a sober commentary from the Pentagon and then it switches to the State Department. They gave the government an hour of free propaganda time. They all knew it, and that's why they had their bureaus there. Nobody pointed out that this was the first time in history that a bombing was scheduled for prime-time television.

ANDRE VLTCHEK

Something similar was happening during the bombing of Belgrade, later.

NOAM CHOMSKY

There they bombed the television tower and some of the human rights groups criticized that, and they said, "well, you know, it was legitimate because it was a propaganda agency. They were providing news."

Actually that also happened in Fallujah. Remember, when the U.S. invaded, the first thing that the marines did when they broke into Fallujah was to take over the general hospital. And they threw all the patients on the floor and tied them up. Somebody raised a question about the Geneva Convention, and the military reported that the hospital was a propaganda agency because it was distributing casualty figures and so therefore we had a right to smash it up. The press repeated it, no comment that I found.

Radiation levels in Fallujah are now reported to be about the same as Hiroshima—whatever weapons they used have left very heavy damages.

ANDRE VLTCHEK

All over Iraq, actually; in several places the radiation is supposed to be fatal. It went up to some unbelievable levels. People are remarkably credible of official propaganda in the West. As someone who was raised in Eastern Europe, I know that there was absolutely no trust amongst the population towards the official government's story, so in a way, the awareness of the people about the world and what was happening in their country was extremely high.

They knew all about the "crimes" allegedly committed by their own system; although not necessarily about much more gruesome crimes that have been committed by the West. Their views were mostly shaped by the Western propaganda, by which they were bombarded for decades, through the radio and television stations. It is worth noting that East Europeans were not brainwashed by Soviet propaganda, but by the Western one. But still, there was interest and some awareness about what's going on in the rest of the world. When I came to the States in 1985, I was at Columbia University, at the film school, and there was the bombing of Libya. And of course Columbia University students were very critical, but then you went to the streets and what shocked me was that total lack of awareness or criticism from the general public. I found that East Europeans were much better informed about their problems, and much more critical of their own system, than the people were here in the United States or in Western Europe.

After living on all the continents of the world, I actually believe that the "Westerners" are the most indoctrinated, the least informed and critical group of people anywhere on earth, of course with some exceptions, like Saudi Arabia. But they believe the opposite: that they are the best informed, and the "freest" people.

NOAM CHOMSKY

There were a couple of interesting studies bearing on that in the late 1970s. There were studies done by Russian research centers in several universities in combination with the government, studying émigrés, trying to figure out where they got their information when they were in Russia. And it was remarkable. Their conclusion was that most Russians, a very high percentage, were listening to the BBC.

ANDRE VLTCHEK

Of course. They were going out of their way to get information from "the other side." I grew up in Pilsen, which is close to the border with Bavaria, and so it was very easy to pick up Western television and radio. The Cold War was in full swing, but foreign television stations were not jammed in Communist Czechoslovakia. If you spoke German you didn't have a problem. The BBC was not jammed. No English-language broadcast was jammed, no matter where it came from. And people in that part of the world spoke or at least understood several languages.

NOAM CHOMSKY

The BBC had a Russian broadcast as well.

ANDRE VLTCHEK

The BBC was usually not jammed in any language, especially not in English. Periodically the Voice of America was jammed in the local languages, or the openly propagandist Radio Liberty/Radio Free Europe. But thinking about it, there was a tremendous thirst for information, and Western propaganda media outlets were taking full advantage of that fact. They had better packaging of their news programs; their propaganda was subtle, refined by centuries of experience. Even when honest, passionate ideological reporting was produced by East Europeans, such as the one concerning the Vietnam War or U.S.-sponsored Contras in Nicaragua, it was so clumsy compared to the refined lies coming from the West, that nobody would believe it in Prague, Budapest, even in certain circles in Moscow. When I came to the United States, I was actually shocked by how misinformed I was by Western propaganda.

You see the paradox: the West which claims to be free and open and democratic had hardly any access to, and it was not influenced by, the propaganda that was created in the old Soviet Union or now in China. And not only propaganda: most Western European and U.S. citizens are not influenced by the way Soviets or Chinese see the world. They don't know much about it. Their world is mono-polar. They don't compare different ideas, ideals, and ideologies. They only have one ideology; which can be called "market-fundamentalism," and is served by multi-party Parliamentary systems or by the constitutional monarchies. But the former Soviets and the Chinese were, and are, well informed about capitalism, about Western views on Communism. So who is more open and who is better informed? Look at Chinese bookstores: plenty of capitalist literature.

Look at U.S. or European bookstores: hardly any Communist Chinese literature.

So this is what I am arguing, when I am writing for the *People's Daily* in China and for *China Daily*, when they interview me now, frequently, in the Chinese media. I am arguing that they should actually be very aware and very careful about the Western propaganda targeting their country. I told them, it's not really there to inform you, it's to break the country.

And that's why I am very, very wary about countries like Cuba or China that are under siege, fully opening their cyberspace and media. I am afraid that all this damaging Western propaganda would enter which is actually geared to break the country as it was geared to break Czechoslovakia, as it was geared to break the Soviet Union. So it's not that I am defending censorship, but on the other hand I also know how vicious and deadly Western airwaves and websites can be. Their main goal is to hurt, to destroy, and not to inform.

Whatever we read about China, whenever people go to China, they are shocked because it is a totally different country from what they imagined from reading Western reports. It is totally different from what we are being told, and what the Chinese people are being told about their own nation, by our mass media and propaganda system. It's very complex.

NOAM CHOMSKY

It is. And there has been a century of intense ... a very sophisticated effort to develop a complex propaganda system. Mostly it's used to brainwash people here through advertising. Huge amounts of capital go into marketing and advertising, and it's basically to maintain a consumer society. For example, some years ago advertisers realized that there is a segment of

7   Art district, Beijing, China. (Copyright Andre Vltchek)

the population that they are not reaching, because they don't have any money, namely children. And a lot of thinking was done about what to do with this and they developed propaganda aimed at infants to try to get them to nag their parents because that's where the money is. So if the children can demand from their parents, that they want this or that, parents would get it for them.

And there is now an academic discipline, taught at applied psychology departments, of nagging. Different kinds of nagging for different kinds of purposes. If you ever watch television as I sometimes do with my grandchildren, from two years old they are being bombarded with consumer messages. There is nothing left untouched. So when they turned to foreign propaganda, they've got all the techniques.

I think one person who was really impressed by this was Goebbels. He wrote that he modeled the German Nazi propaganda on American commercial advertising, which is at its best quite sophisticated.

ANDRE VLTCHEK

It's exactly what I wanted to say: advertising is propaganda and vice versa. In a way, propaganda is an effort to advertise, to sell a certain political or economic system, to promote one particular world vision. It does not have to only promote vacuum cleaners....

NOAM CHOMSKY

Yes. It is also interesting that nobody mentions one very obvious fact about advertising—it is designed to undermine the market. If you take an economics course, you learn that markets are based on informed consumers making rational choices. Take a look at a television ad.; it is designed to create uninformed consumers making irrational choices. So you've got this immense contradiction staring you right in the face. We are supposed to love markets. We have grand theories, economists, and the Federal Reserve trying to preserve markets. And yet there is a huge industry devoted to undermining them and it's right in front of your eyes but none of these contradictions can be seen. Actually they do the same with elections. The goal of elections now is to undermine democracy. They are run by the public relations industry and they're certainly not trying to create informed voters who'll make rational choices. They are trying to delude people into making irrational choices. The same techniques that are used to undermine markets are used to undermine democracy. It's one of the major industries in the country and its basic workings are invisible.

ANDRE VLTCHEK

Has the U.S. media got worse since the 1950s and 1960s? Wasn't it a little bit more diverse then?

NOAM CHOMSKY

If you look as far back as the 1930s, there was quite a range of newspapers, and there was a radical press. By the 1950s it had become more commercialized and unquestioning, though there were still about 800 labor newspapers, sometimes quite critical and militant, reaching maybe 30 million people. But the mainstream press was highly conformist. Take the coup in Iran—the *New York Times* editorial praised the coup and saw it as a great thing that they threw out Mosaddegh in 1953. He was vilified in the American press—a "crazy man" walking around in pajamas and crying, a "lunatic Arab." Some probably didn't know that Persians weren't Arabs. The *Times* editors said this coup will be an object lesson to other leaders who "go berserk with radical nationalism" and try to take control of their own resources. This will teach them; this all leads the way to more responsible leaders who will not behave like this strayed one, nationalizing their own resources and taking them away from us.

And it was the same with the Guatemalan coup the next year. Edward Bernays, the great guru of public relations, was hired by the United Fruit Company to give fake stories to the press, like the Communist takeover, another step toward Communist world conquest, and so on. Later the public relations officer at United Fruit wrote a memoir about it. He was asked afterward, when the story came out: "Didn't you think there was something strange about giving this material to the press?" He said, "Not really, because they were so eager for it. So we just gave it to them."

ANDRE VLTCHEK

I came to New York in 1985 and I was actually very impressed. My life in the United States centered on Manhattan, which was extremely diverse intellectually. I would go to the East Village and there were Shining Path or MRTA bookstores. I couldn't believe it—I was in the center of the Empire and there were all these guerrilla movements running their bookstores with the publications printed in the U.S. or imported from abroad. Maoists and other leftists from India also had their own publications and bookstores. These institutions were also functioning like some public, gathering places. But then, after the internet era began, somehow everything disappeared. I don't find these bookstores anymore, anywhere in New York. I asked my friends who still live there and they say it's all gone. New York increasingly resembles the rest of the country.

NOAM CHOMSKY

Part of much more general phenomena. Many factors. Been going on for a long time. When I was roaming the secondhand bookstores near Union Square, New York, 70-plus years ago, the variety was far wider and in my view intellectually much richer than what you describe in the '80s.

ANDRE VLTCHEK

Even in Europe, in Paris, in the past you would go to some café and it would be next to a newsstand, and you would have

Communist newspapers sitting in front of you and there would be *Le Monde* and there would be the conservative *Le Figaro* and maybe some fascist stuff, too… all for a good measure. And you could just sit down, sip your coffee and just looking at headlines, you could get an idea of what the left and the right are saying and you could buy two to three newspapers. None of that is there anymore. It is there in a few places in Paris, but not nearly so prevalent.

NOAM CHOMSKY

Also, *Le Monde* is nothing like what it was in the 1960s and 1970s. There is much less serious independent reporting and inquiry and sources have sharply reduced. Just check the number of news bureaus abroad, and the sources used by what used to be quality local journals with their own sources not many years ago.

ANDRE VLTCHEK

But what replaced it is the internet. I spoke on the issue at Sydney University recently, and in Auckland. Let's see if we can agree on this. What I have been saying is that the internet consolidated the official right-wing story around the front page. So if you open, for instance, Yahoo… most people of course don't know what they are searching for. All the information is there, but you have to be very determined….

NOAM CHOMSKY

You have to know what you are looking for.

ANDRE VLTCHEK

Exactly. You have to be knowledgeable. You have to improvise during your search.

NOAM CHOMSKY

Just as you can't walk into the New York Public Library and say I want to be a biologist. Everything's there but it wouldn't do you any good.

ANDRE VLTCHEK

Exactly! So actually the situation as I see it is that it is good for people like us, it is also good for researchers who know exactly what they are looking for, but if you are just a person who wants to read alternative interpretation of news, he or she would probably be led in a very dubious direction.

NOAM CHOMSKY

You would get totally confused, yes. I'm glad that it's there all the time, if it's used for good purposes. But if anyone studies the general effects, I think they would find that mostly it confuses people and drives them into sects or cults. It is easy to start a cult on the internet. Suppose you and I decided to spread the belief that President Obama is the anti-Christ. First of all, 25 percent of the Republicans apparently believe it already, but we could start posting things and somebody else would post something else and pretty soon you would have a following and people would think why not? You know, I mean, why not believe that, why believe what they say on different pages that are all lies anyway, so I'll believe this. And you have major cults developing which just draw people away from the real issues, from serious activism. I mean, take the huge 9/11 Truth Movement—its major impact has been to draw off energy from trying to do anything about the problems that have arisen. It's easier to sit at the internet and to work through some technical article you don't understand about whether there are nanothermite traces found in the building WTC-7. It's easier to do that than organizing protests against the Iraq War—a lot easier.

That particular movement is a pretty striking phenomenon. It has quite a lot of outreach. I mean, I wouldn't be surprised if maybe a third of the population thinks it's sort of credible. So maybe a third of the population thinks we are governed by homicidal maniacs who want to murder us all. Well, ok, now go back to work, you can't do anything about it so it's out of my hands.

I don't think we can just attribute this to the existence of the internet. At least in the U.S., it's part of a general decline of faith in institutions, almost any institutions. And that traces to factors much deeper and pervasive than the internet.

ANDRE VLTCHEK

It is a very interesting subject that you are raising. Conspiracy theories are also closely linked to doomsday and disaster films. I think that much commercial film and fiction is desensitizing people to the point that while they still see, periodically, the reality around them, when they compare it to the virtual reality with which they are bombarded day and night, like some horrible insects destroying their country, or half of California falling off the cliff, of course all these things that they are facing in real life appear to be banal and really not too important. Real wars, hunger, plunder of resources in faraway places, homelessness, and lack of democracy: all banal. And then the conspiracy theory about 9/11 would connect to that too. Reality as you said is much more demanding—you have to be determined, you have to call for demonstrations, you have to organize people, to resist, to rebel.

NOAM CHOMSKY

Sounds to me very plausible. And we can add that it's risky too—there is nothing risky about talking to your friends over the internet.

ANDRE VLTCHEK

Yes, and the ideas of the 9/11 Truth Movement have spread across the world. I see them in Istanbul; I see them in South America. They are basically taken for granted even by some groups of very educated people. Claiming that the U.S. government didn't blow up the World Trade Center, saying it somewhere among the intellectuals in Istanbul would make one totally boring and mainstream.

NOAM CHOMSKY

Regarding the U.S. phenomenon in particular, there is a good book by a literary critic, H. Bruce Franklin, who did a study of American popular literature from colonial times up to the present modern period, to include television and so on. And he's found some quite interesting things. One thing that he found is that there is a common theme running through the literature, a little bit like what you have described: "We are on the edge of an impending catastrophe, and there is some incredible enemy who's just about to overwhelm and destroy us. And in the last minute we're saved by a super weapon or some superhero which rises up."

In more recent years, it is things like this that appear on television—Russians are conquering the country, high school students go to the hills and they organize and fight off the invaders and that kind of thing. And who's the enemy? Quite typically it's someone we are crushing. So in the early stages it's the Indians. In the Declaration of Independence Thomas Jefferson gives his condemnation of King George III saying he unleashed against us "the merciless Indian savages, whose known way of warfare, is an undistinguished destruction of all ages, sexes and conditions." And Jefferson was there—he knew perfectly well it was merciless European savages—but I don't think he was lying. The conception was: "here we are peaceful... the merciless savages are reacting to our takeover of their lands and our driving them out and our killing them by merciless means." The same enemy is there right throughout the conquest of the new territory.

Later it becomes the fear of a slave revolt—the slaves are going to rise up, they are going to kill all the men, and rape all the women, and take over—but we are saved at the last minute. Later in the century, interestingly, it becomes the Chinese—Chinese coolies as they were called were kidnapped and brought to the United States to build the railroads and they would open laundries and things like that, and a theme in literature was: they are going to take over, they have insidious plans, hundreds of millions of them, they were planning to work themselves into American society and take it over.

There was a novel, I think it may have been by Jack London, a progressive writer, saying that we should kill everyone in China with biological warfare to stop them before they take over. Later, in the 1950s, it's the Red Chinese trying to poison American youth, pouring drugs into the country to take it over that way. During the Vietnam War, a myth developed that the army is being hooked on drugs... there is an element of truth to it, because they were really pretty angry about what was going on, depressed and so on, but it turns out that they were mostly taking alcohol. But what was focused on was drugs and this was an insidious Vietnamese/Red Chinese plot to turn our brave young men into hardened criminals and drug addicts. So when they came back to the United States they kind of tear the place to shreds. And that's a large part of what lay behind the propaganda for the drug war. And it goes on like that right to the present—now it's the Islamic fascists who may take over. Half of the people who call themselves Republicans think that Obama is trying to impose *sharia* law, and not just on the United States but on the entire world.

4

The Soviet Bloc

NOAM CHOMSKY

I am interested in hearing what you've got to say about Eastern Europe.

ANDRE VLTCHEK

Eastern Europe depresses me. At some point in history, the people of countries like Czechoslovakia, Hungary, East Germany were forced to do something really right for humanity, but they did it against their will, and so in my opinion they ended up dreaming for all those decades how to join the oppressors. And over the last two decades they are living that dream. Some of them do, not all; but at least their elites. There are all these myths about Eastern Europe, about how bad things were there. East and Central European dissidents are like holy cows. You can't discuss intellectuals and writers like Václav Havel or Milan Kundera. They can't be criticized, can't be touched. They were serving the West, one-sidedly.

The reason I wanted to come back to this topic is because this is actually one of the first issues that you and I discussed when we first met many years ago and when we began corresponding. We were writing about how much more brutal the regimes were in the Western colonies than in the Soviet satellites.

NOAM CHOMSKY

The only place I have been to in that part of the world is Hungary and I wasn't there long, but I did meet with a lot of their dissidents and they were just super neo-liberal, awed by everything they saw in the West, by every idea coming from there, as if since it wasn't Russia, it has to be good, you know. This was just a couple years ago. They were nice people. We agreed on a lot of things, but their uncritical love of Western ideas was shocking to me.

ANDRE VLTCHEK

I just went to *Escuela Mecanica* in Buenos Aires, and I went to this enormous Museum of Memory and Human Rights in Santiago de Chile—*Museo de la memoria y los derechos humanos*—it's tremendous. This museum shows all the horrors that were done

8   Colombian artist Francisco Botero's Abu Ghraib series of paintings on display at the Museum of Memory and Human Rights, Santiago, Chile. (Copyright Andre Vltchek)

to Chile and also to other Latin American countries. I saw some stunning work by Botero—the most important contemporary Colombian sculptor. His canvases depict the torture of Muslim people at Abu Graib prison in Baghdad by U.S. soldiers. It was so powerful! I was impressed: a great Colombian sculptor and a great Chilean museum showing solidarity, extending hands to Arab people. You could never even imagine something like that in Eastern Europe.

As a child, I spent several dreadful years in Czechoslovakia. My years were dreadful, not because Czechoslovakia was Communist, but because my mother was half Chinese and half Russian, and she actually looked Asian, so I had to face terrible racism there.

Without being too cynical, Moscow's invasion of 1968 to put down the Prague Spring was not necessarily something that should have happened and it broke the spine of their "socialism with a human face" but there was no massacre performed by the Soviets; few people fell under the tanks. Most of what happened was accidents; some people who died were drunk.

NOAM CHOMSKY

If it happened in Latin America, nobody would even notice it.

ANDRE VLTCHEK

Exactly! More people died in Grenada. In Prague, it was surgical. There were no rapes. There was no torture. They kept the borders open for several months, so people who wanted to leave had their choice. My father, who was a nuclear scientist, had an offer from Canada to get out; he never left. Before 1968 he was a member of the Communist Party of Czechoslovakia. He threw his membership card in the face of some official and left the Party. Nothing happened. He continued working, although it probably prevented him from taking trips abroad and from promotion. But can you imagine, if this happened in El Salvador or in Greece during the U.S.-backed military regime, or in Indonesia after 1965, or Chile after 1973? My entire family would have been wiped out, perhaps after direct orders from Washington.

And people like Kundera, Havel, and Kohout knew it. But they opted to become intellectual stars by showing only one side of the story. Have you ever read anything by Kundera that would comment on the horrors that the U.S. or Europe put the rest of the world through? And after writing one cheap sentimental propaganda novel after another, he was elevated by the critics to the level of serious literature.

NOAM CHOMSKY

Actually it's known to scholarship—it has been repeatedly pointed out that compared to Latin America, in the post-Stalin era, East Europe's repression was mild. In fact it's kind of striking but the Soviet Union actually subsidized Eastern Europe so that it ended up richer than Russia. The Soviet Empire is the only empire in history where the imperial center was poorer than the colonies.

ANDRE VLTCHEK

Yes. And it was evidently poorer. I knew it from childhood. My grandmother was in Leningrad, in St. Petersburg, while I grew up in Czechoslovakia. I was born in Leningrad, but my parents took me to Czecholsovakia. My mother would basically send me back to Russia to see my grandmother every summer for three months. I loved Russia, counted the days to go back, every year. But I also experienced as a child this contrast between Czechoslovakia and the Soviet Union. Leningrad was one of the richest cities in the Soviet Union, but even then it was very clear that occupied Czechoslovakia was allowed to remain much wealthier than the USSR. The Soviets didn't really do anything about the disparities. They didn't suck everything out of the country as we do. They could have, but they didn't. Of course, the Soviet Union never got any credit for this; from the West or from East European intellectuals.

NOAM CHOMSKY

Being part of the Soviet Empire—it might have had unpleasant reasons but the facts are pretty clear. And they are known to scholarship too, but no one draws any conclusions from them.

ANDRE VLTCHEK

I think what is totally being forgotten is the tremendous amount of good things that Eastern Europe actually did for the world. As we established earlier, East Europeans were supporting liberation struggles all over the world; they were supporting Vietnam during the American War. They were helping tens of millions in Africa, the Middle East, everywhere. Russians had huge publishing houses that were printing books for the poorest nations on earth, in their own languages.

My Indian friends told me that they were growing up on subsidized CDs of classical music produced by the *Melodiya* state record company. I can't even recount what these countries did for the world. I mean, my two Czech uncles on my father's side, they were building everything from sugar mills to steel mills in the Middle East, in Africa and in Southeast Asia. It was not like some kind of a forced labor, these people were earning hard currency for their tough labor, but it was still internationalist help. What they were doing was tremendous, but what it came down to is that everybody remembers only the fact that it was part of this so-called "Evil Empire." Western propaganda defeated all good intentions.

Many of the East European dissidents came from the elites. For instance, Václav Havel's family used to be one of the richest in Czechoslovakia before the Communists won elections in 1948. They owned everything from real estate to the Barrandov film studio, which is still one of the largest film studios in Eastern Europe. Josef Škvorecký, a dissident writer who ended up teaching in Toronto, was very honest about it. In his novel *The Cowards* he describes the liberation of Czechoslovakia by the Red Army, and he says that those Russians rode horses and smelled and that he would of course much rather have Americans and Brits liberating his land, as he was from the upper middle class and loved jazz.

NOAM CHOMSKY

Were you surprised by the racist outbursts over black footballers in Poland and Ukraine during the Euro 2012 football championships?

ANDRE VLTCHEK

I am not surprised. I think that there has always been racism in Eastern Europe. But I also think that once they got the system which the dissidents and the West were fighting for, many ugly things simply surfaced. Actually, it was little bit like in the Soviet

Union itself. What the Communists did was to force a country that was previously isolated and very backward to suddenly become internationalist. That worked for some, mainly it worked for intellectuals. But the majority of the people remained closed, some even racist.

And you know, the Soviet Union got all those people from Africa, from Southeast Asia, from the Middle East; they opened universities and colleges for them, which again was fantastic. But the normal person on the street probably didn't care much about it. Ordinary Russians didn't understand what was going on, and they were still very chauvinist. It's like in India today— if you could turn India into a Communist country and open schools for Africans, people from the Middle East and other parts of the world, ordinary people would not accept it. My Kenyan friend, a former parliamentarian and a closet Marxist, studied in India. He is black. He told me that he was treated well at the university, but once he got to the streets of New Delhi, children came running to him, often asking: "Uncle, where is your tail? Do you live on the trees?" There is simply not enough education, and not enough acceptance of other cultures. Soviets put their country on the vanguard of the fight against imperialism, racism, and discrimination. But a huge sector of the population was not ready for it, it resisted, it remained racist. I think that was the case, not only in the former USSR, but also all over Eastern Europe. Then, once the system that was promoting egalitarianism collapsed, all those terrible oppressed bigotries surfaced again.

NOAM CHOMSKY

How would you assess the rise of the far right parties in Eastern Europe?

ANDRE VLTCHEK

I think they are going to be in Eastern Europe as they are in Denmark, as they are in Holland, Greece and elsewhere. I think that Europe as a whole is historically fascist and it has demonstrated this by plundering the entire planet for centuries, and on top of this it is culturally and economically defunct, a declining continent.

In the past Europe has demonstrated unmatchable brutality through genocides, which we have already described, through the massacres when they were colonial masters of the world, and they are still aiming at controlling the world now, together with their trigger-happy senior partner. Therefore I am not surprised: I think that perhaps the fascist parties are something quite natural for Europe and I find it easier to fight them when they surface, than those egotistic systems that Europe had after World War II, which created great social nets for Europeans at the expense of starving billions all over the world.

NOAM CHOMSKY

Do you think there are prospects for socialism in Eastern Europe?

ANDRE VLTCHEK

I think in Russia, Ukraine, and to some extent in Bulgaria, there is great nostalgia for Communism or socialism. It is not only a matter of a political or economic system. I think now that many people in the former USSR feel an emptiness; life somehow lost its meaning. The goals of the USSR were lofty and some of them were very impressive: freedom for all poor parts of the world, anti-colonialism, anti-imperialism, social justice.

It is interesting that both young and old generations are now listening to the old Soviet-era tunes, over and over again. Modern literature is reflecting the void that emerged after the collapse of the country. But the Russian Communist Party is sclerotic and disoriented. I don't think Russia is yet at the stage when it could define a path that might lead back to socialism or Russian-style Communism. It is a very confused society, not as confident as China. It feels defeated, fragmented, and full of uncertainties. However, I think that the Russian soul is essentially socialist. I would not be surprised if Russia redefines itself as a socialist country within the next decade or two.

Most Eastern and Central European countries will never go back to socialism, I think. They are now part of the regime; they are integrated to the Western structures. And like people in Western Europe: they would never be allowed to change their system again. It seems to be a one-way street, unless there is some global revolution.

When I was living in Pilsen, except for people like Havel, Kundera or Kohout or those people in Czechoslovakia who were really from the hardcore opposition, the majority of folks were dreaming about what they had immediately before and during 1968. They were dreaming about what they called socialism with a human face—which was probably a very good concept, at least in Czechoslovakia. It worked there. Although you know what, nobody wants to admit? It is that China today is much more open than Czechoslovakia was in 1968, before the Soviet invasion. It is easier to get a passport, to cross the border; there is a greater variety of political opinions in the bookstores in Beijing now than there was in Prague in 1968.

However, now when you talk to Czech people, the majority of them are complaining; but they were always complaining, so I don't take it too seriously, even now. The majority of Czech people think that the Czechoslovak Communist system was not good, the post-Communist system is not good, but they don't do anything about it, nothing to change it. There is not much talk about reintroducing Dubček's socialism with a human face. However the Czech Communist Party is the third most powerful political party in the country.

NOAM CHOMSKY

How do they stand on social and economic issues?

ANDRE VLTCHEK

The Communist Party there is quite timid. To my taste it is not very outspoken; it is too busy trying to prove to Czechs and to the world that it became a "normal," "constitutional" political force. It is definitely not a revolutionary party. You see, the Czech Republic is in a way a little bit like Chile. Twenty years after Pinochet, Chile is back to its social democratic, pre-1973 mode, no matter who is sitting in La Moneda, the Presidential Palace. Czechs were always in essence social democrats, too. That's why it was unique in what used to be called the Soviet Bloc. The country has a very good social system no matter who governs it.

Historically, even in the days of Austro-Hungarian Empire, it was the richest part because of its raw materials, heavy industry, and work ethic. So then this so called First Republic—the one that existed between World Wars I and II—was a strictly social democratic country, and one could say it was a decent country. Even Sartre was impressed when he came to visit: he saw working-class people rowing the boats and having picnics on Sunday with their families. Of course it was not perfect, as there was some serious discrimination of ethnic minorities, but it was decent compared to the rest of Europe of the same historic period.

Czechoslovakia, or the Czech Republic, was never too much to the left, but I think that if we compare the Czech Republic to what we see in the rest of the world right now, it still stands somewhere decently in the centre left, but not much further. But the fact that the country doesn't want to deal with foreign policy, and that it is such a close ally of the United States, is disturbing. So, on the one hand it is a social democracy with an admirable safety net, but on the other, when it comes to foreign policy the country sends its military units to Iraq and Afghanistan.

NOAM CHOMSKY

And is there a fear of Russia?

ANDRE VLTCHEK

No. There is absolutely no fear of Russia.

NOAM CHOMSKY

So, what is the driving force for their foreign policy?

ANDRE VLTCHEK

Centuries of being used to collaborating with whoever is in charge at the time. I tell Czechs to their face: in many ways what they are doing right now is collaboration. It is not much different from what they were doing during the Austro-Hungarian Empire, World War II Nazi occupation, or during the occupation by the Soviet Union.

NOAM CHOMSKY

Was there a lot of collaboration during World War II under the German occupation?

ANDRE VLTCHEK

Of course! Czechoslovakia at that time was broken into two parts. The Czech lands were overrun by Germany; they were part of Nazi Germany after the Sudetenland annexation and consequent occupation. Slovakia at that time was its own independent fascist country.

NOAM CHOMSKY

But there was a partisan movement.

ANDRE VLTCHEK

There was a partisan movement in Slovakia, but mainly towards the end of the war. In the Czech part they had very weak resistance. There was the assassination of Reinhard Heydrich (Deputy Reich-Protector of Bohemia and Moravia) in 1942. This was executed by a British-trained team of Czech and Slovak soldiers who had been sent by the Czechoslovak government-in-exile to kill him, which led to retaliation by Germans and mass murder in Lidice and Ležáky, two villages that were leveled with the ground, but that was probably the only act of strong resistance, and they say that it was orchestrated from Britain because there was embarrassingly almost no resistance inside the country.

NOAM CHOMSKY

It was actually opposed by the Czech partisans, because they knew it was going to cause a hideous reaction.

ANDRE VLTCHEK

Exactly. The people who executed it were actually airlifted from the UK.

NOAM CHOMSKY

But the main partisan activities were in Slovakia?

ANDRE VLTCHEK

Yes. The Czech lands at that time had some of the greatest, most powerful industry in the world. For instance, Skoda in the city of Pilsen was one of the greatest producers of arms, on a par with the German conglomerate Krupp. During the occupation the Czechs were working very closely with the German military complex. It was actually the Americans who liberated the Western part of the Bohemia, around Pilsen, but before they did so, they bombed the Skoda works to the ground. Part of the reason was because it was one of the biggest military factories working for Germans, but probably the main reason was that the U.S. knew that all of Czechoslovakia would end up in the Eastern zone at the end of the war, so they wanted to cause as much damage as possible.

But about the collaboration, my father told me that the first thing that the Germans did when they came to the Czech lands was to cancel all debts, mortgages, and loans that Czech families had with the banks. The Germans expected that Czechs would become close collaborators, so the first thing they did was to win their hearts and minds—and what could be a better way to do it in the heart of Europe than by offering financial incentives.

NOAM CHOMSKY

It is very interesting topic, the collaboration in Europe... I was looking at various countries and records of collaboration and I couldn't find anything about Holland, so I asked Hans Koning, who was a resister during World War II inside Holland. He said that there was virtually no collaboration in Holland, with the Germans. And it seemed to me extremely surprising, so I asked him to explain. He said he happened to be going back to Amsterdam the next summer and he would consult with a friend of his who runs the war museum there.

When he came back in the fall, he told me what his friend had told him and showed him. In fact there was a secret archive, kept from the public, which had in it the information about the Dutch collaboration with the Nazis. He said that to his surprise it was quite extensive. I happened to mention this to a Dutch linguist friend afterward, and he just laughed. He told me his relatives were collaborating with the Nazis. But it's suppressed, as you know.

ANDRE VLTCHEK

This makes me think that we should always remember that when we talk about World War II; there were clear divisions. At the end of the war, Europe was not only divided between Eastern and Western Blocs, but also between those countries that won and those that lost the war. That's also not discussed by official media outlets and by official history books, but several countries of Eastern Europe actually lost the war. Slovakia, Hungary, Romania, Bulgaria—they were not really liberated, just as East Germany was not. All of these countries were actually defeated. They were fighting on the side of the Nazis.

We are talking about countries which just over a decade earlier were overpowered as fascist states, which participated in one of the most horrible projects in human history. The Soviet Union lost tens of millions of people fighting and defeating fascism. Western propaganda only talks about those poor Hungarians who fought the Soviets and lost their lives in Budapest in the 1950s, but what about the sensitivities and fears of the Soviet people, what about their fear that they could once again have to face a fascist monster on their border?

It appears to me that there is no serious discussion in the West about the Soviet past from angles other than the official one. It is emphasized that the Soviet Union was some kind of criminal country that was violating human rights relentlessly and continuously. I was looking at the past between the two wars in some detail. I have some personal stakes: my grandfather was a member of the Soviet government and he was executed in the 1930s in a purge. Of course my family suffered tremendously and the issue was always a very painful one. However, living on all six continents and studying the past, I realized that, especially in the light of the research that is being done now in Russia but also in China and elsewhere, first of all, there were not tens of millions of people who died for political reasons under Stalin.

There were plenty of people, but the camps were mainly labor camps. There were also rapists, there were mass killers, common criminals, all mixed with political prisoners. The revolution was tough, but the Tsarist Empire was appalling and feudal and had to be smashed. Stalin did some terrible things, but it is wrong to take him out of historic context. If we agree that each human life has the same value no matter where it is, what color people are, then looking at the same historic period, we can see absolutely outrageous genocidal excesses of colonialism performed by European nations under so called constitutional monarchies or under so called multi-party democracies. The idea of totally rejecting Soviet-style or other Communist systems just based on the massacres committed in that period of time would also mean that we would have to ban as inhuman and genocidal the constitutional monarchies and so called multi-party western democracies. British, Belgian, Dutch, German, French, and other Western nations in Africa, Asia, the Middle East and elsewhere slaughtered incomparably more people than in the Soviet Union in the same historic period. However, such a comparison is hardly ever allowed to be made.

The so-called collapse of the Soviet Union was a collapse of pluralism in many ways. It is not to say that the system was worth following blindly, or that Stalinism was a great set of values. However, there were some ideas that led to positive changes in the world, including determined opposition to colonialism and to Western imperialism. Many countries worldwide would still be colonies if not for the help their liberation movements received from the Soviet Union.

NOAM CHOMSKY

You can't look at it, for the same reason that you can't compare what happened to Latin American dissidents with East European dissidents. It would undermine the entire groundwork; the underpinnings of the entire ideology, of policy of image and everything else. It would tear everything to shreds.

ANDRE VLTCHEK

There are many topics that are taboo in the West and its colonies. I will tell you one short story. I was living in Hanoi and one day an old gentleman from Afghanistan, an educator, came to visit. He was on an official visit to UNESCO. We were introduced and I spent two afternoons taking him around Hanoi. At one point we were sitting in a café and I asked him, "How was Afghanistan during the Soviet Union?" and he said, "Look, it was the only time that my country had any hope. This is when the teachers were both men and women, and women had the same rights as men; and when the country was actually developing for its people." I said "But this is not what we read!" And he said, "Of course, it's not what you are going to read but..." He gave me many examples and we ended up talking for two days.

He's not the only person who was enthusiastic about the pro-Soviet era in Afghanistan. I talked to other people later, mostly their educators, and now I am convinced that even the Soviet involvement in Afghanistan was totally different from what we are told through the mass media in the West.

NOAM CHOMSKY

Well, the Soviet period in Afghanistan was pretty horrible, but there is a lot more to say about it than appears here. The United Nations had a representative in Kabul in the '80s working on women's rights, a well-known international feminist. She was one of the women who organized International Women's Day. Towards the end she wrote a couple of articles about the state of women in Kabul under the Russians, and it was a very positive picture. She said the only real problem they had was Hekmatyar and the rest of the U.S.-backed Islamist extremists who were throwing acid in their faces. But other than that, they were very free. They wore what they liked, went to college and had opportunities. I think she sent the article to the *Washington Post*, which refused to print it. Then, more interestingly, she sent it to the major feminist journal in the United States and they refused to print it. Finally it was printed in the *Asia Times*, or somewhere like that.

ANDRE VLTCHEK

It was not only women who apparently benefited; the state of education also was quite good. There were new schools being built. Health and the infrastructure improved.

NOAM CHOMSKY

I think the most dramatic case is Cuba. It's right in front of our eyes, you know. And the United States has been carrying out a major war against Cuba for 50 years: economic warfare, a long series of serious terrorist attacks, and the only thing that can be said about Cuba is how awful it is. And whatever you think about Cuba, there are some pretty remarkable achievements. Health, for example, is unbelievable!

ANDRE VLTCHEK

But of course! Also education and culture.

NOAM CHOMSKY

And the other thing is Cuba's role in Africa. Cuba had played a huge role in liberating Africa.

ANDRE VLTCHEK

Yes. Che Guevara brought an entire black contingent from Cuba to fight for the liberation of Congo.

NOAM CHOMSKY

Yes, but also the Cuban involvement in Angola and Namibia. They basically drove out the South Africans. And they did it in a completely selfless way. They never took any credit for it. They never even wanted to be known. They wanted the African leaders to be able to take credit for it. And it was a tremendous achievement—not only the liberation, but even the way they broke the psychological stranglehold. There was a kind of feeling around Africa, both among blacks and whites, that white mercenaries can't be defeated. But Cuba sent in black soldiers, they drove the South African forces out of Angola, and they later liberated Namibia and that gave a tremendous psychological shock all over the whole continent, and they—the Cubans— played the major role in the liberation.

ANDRE VLTCHEK

Cuba is a true internationalist society, and the work that I see their doctors are doing all over the world, from Oceania to Latin America to Africa, is remarkable. I just wrote a long article about Cochabamba [Bolivia] where they were involved. I saw them in action in places like Kiribati [Oceania], in the middle of nowhere. They are very kind, very dedicated.

NOAM CHOMSKY

In Haiti they had been incredible. Also, after the Pakistan flood of 2010, there's been a lot of talk about how the West sent doctors and how they have been wonderful, but the main ones were Cubans and the Cubans didn't stay in the towns, they went off to the difficult, hard places and they stayed there, unlike the Westerners. The Westerners pulled out, and you can read that in the press in India and you can read it in the press in Pakistan, but try to find it here.

Actually I had an interesting experience in South Africa when I was there in the early 1990s. I happened to be there just at the time when a contingent of Cuban doctors came in. The reaction was extremely interesting. The white doctors had left but there were black doctors who were very angry about the new arrivals. I asked one of the officials in the Health Ministry, how come the black doctors are objecting to the Cubans coming in? He said: because the Cubans shamed them—the Cubans go off into the poor rural villages and the rising new black doctors want to live in luxury in the cities.

ANDRE VLTCHEK

And you know what Cuban doctors did in South Africa? They learned the local languages and dialects. This is another thing which is remarkable about them, because while the local doctors were speaking Afrikaner or English, often not being able to communicate with the local population, Cuban doctors came and the first thing they did was learn the local language.

NOAM CHOMSKY

Yes. And they integrate with the people, which is truly remarkable. I think Cuban medical expenses are a tiny fraction of U.S. medical expenses but their health levels are about the same.

ANDRE VLTCHEK

Of course. Their system is based on preventive medicine. It is very symbolic—their achievements in medicine—because this is one way how they can help the world, and they are doing it everywhere, no matter what problems they have at home. I saw them in action even in rich Chile, right after the last major earthquake. In Rancagua they had an entire medical tent city run by Cubans.

NOAM CHOMSKY

You probably know they offered to send medical teams to the United States after hurricane Katrina but they were turned down.

5

India and China

ANDRE VLTCHEK

Noam, how do you regard the continuous barrage of anti-Chinese propaganda in almost all mainstream Western media outlets, and the glorification of so-called "Indian democracy?"

NOAM CHOMSKY

If you take a look at mortality rates in Communist China, which are now being pretty closely studied, they dropped very sharply up until about 1979, after which they leveled off during the period of capitalist reforms under Deng Xiao Ping. As we discussed earlier, in democratic capitalist India alone 100 million people died as compared with China under Communism. Amartya Sen who did the research on India which we discussed earlier pointed out that while there were horrible famines in India under British rule right into the early 1940s, after independence there were no more famines, because it was a more democratic system.

India is horrible in many ways, and the horrors there generally go under-reported. Once I was driving through New Delhi with a very committed and dedicated activist friend. We were on our way to a demonstration, where we were both going to speak. But you know when you drive down the street in India, even in New Delhi which is now a rich city by Indian standards, you stop at a street corner and beggars start coming around—a woman with a starving child, asking for a rupee or something. My friend, who is a dedicated activist and gave her life to the struggle, told me "don't give them anything." And I said, "why not?" She said, "well, if you give them one rupee soon we will have a thousand people converging on us." I noticed as we drove she never looked out of the window. I asked her how she could live with this all around her all the time. She said the only way is if you pretend you don't see it, otherwise you kill yourself. You can't survive if you look at it, and most people just choose not to.

ANDRE VLTCHEK

India is often described as a country with tremendous potential but it's still a country which lives in the middle ages in many ways. No major mass media outlet in the West would criticize the Indian system, as it is some awful fusion of feudalism and capitalism, with historic anti-Chinese sentiments; exactly what we need. Their religions, caste system, clannishness, misery; all scream "failed state," but it is never spoken of.

The other day I was talking to a friend, a doctor of Indian blood and a chief physician in a large hospital in Harare, Zimbabwe. He told me: "India was recently bragging about being the first country that imposed sanctions on South Africa, during apartheid." But knowing the structure of Indian society, can you imagine how cynical that move was? With the appalling caste system, and with the feudalism that segregates hundreds of millions of people, India itself is living under terrible apartheid.

On one hand, they have great scientists, writers, and philosophers. On the other hand, that's only a very small percentage of people. The rest is living in a totally feudal environment. I am working on a film about Dalit children in

Tamil Nadu. When you go down there, it's a humbling but also a very shocking experience because you understand all this nonsense about the largest democracy in the world. It's nothing of that nature. It is basically a country where you can still buy an entire block of households to vote in a certain way. You can buy entire villages. You can intimidate entire areas into submission. Some of my Indian friends—intellectuals— are basically there mourning that their country didn't go the Chinese way. Although only a few are tough enough to openly describe what's happening in their country as a total disaster. India is one of the best places to live if you are rich and of upper caste or, better still, both, but what a hell if you are poor or even belonging to what they call the emerging middle class.

NOAM CHOMSKY

India is a huge and complex country, and one thing that is very striking traveling around the country is the difference in mood. In Kerala, people are sitting reading newspapers, there are lively discussions going on, you meet the poorest people and you can talk about things that have to be done, and so on. Objectively it's one of the poorest areas in India, but it is quite different in spirit and character from anything you see on the streets of Delhi, or Calcutta.

ANDRE VLTCHEK

Well, Kerala was run by the Communist Party. But Kerala was a little paradoxical, because on one hand they achieved a really high level of education, but on the other there was a tremendous outflow of skilled workers. So, in fact, instead of staying in Kerala and building the society, many of them went to the Middle East.

NOAM CHOMSKY

That's right. And the state is living on their remittances. It is pathetic driving through Kerala, at least when I was there some years ago. You see this gorgeous agricultural land, rice fields and so on, but things are rotting away.

India is a very exciting country, with many remarkable achievements, but it is one of the most depressing countries I have ever seen. The poverty and the misery are so open and apparent, even compared to Pakistan. My wife and I spent around one month in India and then we went to Pakistan for a week. We happened to go straight from Calcutta to Lahore. In Calcutta we passed through the large market place, where miserable people were begging, dragging their limbs, and trying to drag you to their store. So, yes, I think it was quite ugly. A couple of days later in Lahore we went to the main market place. It's poor, but there was a totally different atmosphere.

9   Slums in Mumbai, India. (Copyright Andre Vltchek)

Before I visited India and Pakistan I talked to Eqbal Ahmad, a very significant Pakistani activist and intellectual who did hugely important work. He was involved with the Algerian FLN, was close to African movements, and involved with the PLO. He did very important work here too: critical scholarship and activism. Ahmad told me that I would discover to my surprise that the press in Pakistan is more free and open than in India. When I went there, I found out that it was true. When he predicted this and I told him that it was hard to believe, he said: "You are missing the point. The press in Pakistan you will be reading was the English press, and that's for a tiny sector of the population. And the dictatorship is perfectly happy to let this tiny sector play their games." He said that if I read the Urdu press I would be appalled.

ANDRE VLTCHEK

Along the same lines, a few years ago two or three of my articles were published by the *Friday Times* in Karachi. It was fine to publish them in English. But when I was invited to come to Pakistan, I could not get a visa. So although of course they would publish me for this small elite, I was not allowed to come to the country and speak.

NOAM CHOMSKY

I knew Najam Sethi, the editor of the *Friday Times*, and his wife: very interesting people. They are quite wealthy and from the Pakistani elite, but he spent time in jail and was tortured. He was then allowed to go back and publish, and he does. They are very brave people but they represent a tiny sector.

ANDRE VLTCHEK

The Indian press is largely provincial and very protective. Some time ago, several progressive journalists from India went to Nepal to publish a magazine called *Himalmag*, which was run by some right-wing businessman called Kunda, and even that was quite left-wing compared to what was done back in India.

NOAM CHOMSKY

Frontline is one of the few exceptions. One of the editors of *Frontline* is a friend. He's an agricultural economist and lived in Tamil Nadu. He took us from Kerala and then through Tamil Nadu right afterward. Two states and strikingly different, although they are right next to each other. Tamil Nadu theoretically is much richer, but Kerala looked much more civilized.

ANDRE VLTCHEK

But back to the topic that we discussed earlier—the number of people who died as a result of the Chinese and Indian political systems. Here we have the two most populous nations on earth, with two distinct cultures and systems. Western propaganda is constantly glorifying India and vilifying China. The so-called Tibet issue never leaves the pages of the newspapers, while Kashmir is hardly mentioned. There is no comparison between the level of brutality in Tibet and Kashmir.

NOAM CHOMSKY

Kashmir is one thing you can't talk about. When I was in India I gave a lot of talks. Somebody asked a question about Kashmir and I just described what you could read in the human rights reports. They got very angry. The next day, at a talk I was giving, there was a very angry demonstration by the Bharatiya Janata Party. After that, the people who invited me insisted that for the rest of the time I was there I should have police protection. Just because I brought up Kashmir.

ANDRE VLTCHEK

And there are other issues you cannot bring up, like the fascist Rashtriya Swayamsevak Sangh (RSS) or National Volunteer Organization. They have even been tailoring their clothes using the *Hitlerjugend* and Italian fascist uniforms as their inspiration.

I was in Gujarat right after the massacres in Ahmedabad. I flew there to investigate the aftermath of the Gujarat massacres and then the Gandhinagar temple standoff. I was there for quite some time. The whole situation was extremely disturbing. I met all those right-wing Hindu elements and organizations, including leaders of the RSS. To my surprise I was warmly invited to talk to the Hindu extremists. I was invited to their homes and offices. I guess I looked sufficiently white to them; "Arian." It felt as if they were burning with desire to share their thoughts and bigoted philosophy with an outsider.

India is full of bigotry. It is also being choked by fundamentalist groups from the two major religions of the country. You cannot leave those groups, you are basically owned by them, you can't escape. It is all endlessly sad; definitely not something that should be presented to the world as an example to follow.

Ahmedabad during the massacres was one of the most shocking places I ever had to cover. The level of violence, of hate, of mercilessness, was just unimaginable. All that killing, plunder, and rape. The mob would attack Muslim houses, slit the bellies of pregnant women. India is an extremely violent country, like Indonesia. But in the West we have a tendency to call these violent countries "peaceful" and "tolerant," as long as they serve as a buffer against China, as long as they plunder their natural resources on behalf of our private companies, as long as they are willing to uphold their savage capitalism. Although in India, unlike in Indonesia, most of the plundering is done by local elites.

NOAM CHOMSKY

The left journalist and activist David Barsamian has been very involved in India. He just recently wanted to return to India, but his visa was denied. The reason was that he had written about Kashmir. He spent time in Kashmir and wrote about it, and that's it: can't get back to India.

ANDRE VLTCHEK

There are many issues one cannot cover in India, such as Kashmir, or the northeast tribal area. One cannot write on the Andaman Islands. There are many topics one simply cannot cover if one wants to return to India at some point. I have to say that I feel much more free working in China. I may be prevented from doing some things, although not to the extent that I am in the West (I was once prevented from filming a public ice-skating rink in Paris, the one in front of the *Hotel de Ville*. When I protested, I was almost arrested).

But in India you can do nothing: no filming or photographing of museums, of government offices, of the metro. You can't even connect to the internet at some five-star hotels, unless you are staying there and they have data on you; unless you fill out several pages and give them your passport so they can copy it. If you apply for a visa, they want to know everything, even the names of your parents, and I think your grandparents, too. They demand that you bring your previous passport with you, and if you don't have it, you have to fill out another set of papers. Security and surveillance are everywhere. It is one of the most oppressive societies I have ever encountered. To the contrary, everything in China feels straightforward: not that they let me stick my lens into the cockpit of a jetfighter. Despite Western propaganda, I think it is one of the easiest countries to work in; incomparable to India.

NOAM CHOMSKY

I have only spent one week in China. I was invited by Peking University to receive an honorary degree. They usually ask you to give a talk; but I was asked to give a political talk, which really shocked me. My friends, who were mostly dissidents, suggested to me that I tone it down because while it won't affect me, it could affect them. So I was not provocative. But one of the questions from the student audience after the talk was, "where do you think China could look to as a model?" I had just been to Taiwan; I took a chance and said, well, you can look at nearby countries like South Korea and Taiwan. That's a really sensitive issue, but there was applause and after that I talked fairly openly.

ANDRE VLTCHEK

I find China an amazing place and I also find it a very interesting model that works very well, at least for them. I am not sure how it could be duplicated anywhere else, but China has raised hundreds of millions of people out of poverty. A lot of propaganda in the West presents China as more capitalist than capitalist countries, a perception with which I totally disagree. Considering that China is not rich—yet—it dedicates huge funds and planning to its social development. I am based, among other places, in Southeast Asia—a bastion of pro-Western savage capitalism. Some countries there have a somehow similar HDI (Human Development Index) to China, and so I don't think we should compare China with France yet, or Beijing with Paris. I compare it with Jakarta, Manila, and Bangkok. I compare the medical system, education, housing, access to drinking water and sanitation, and, of course, the public spaces and public transportation, and the situation in China is so very superior. There are tremendous projects for public transportation—a lot of them are very ecological. Subways, high speed trains, public parks, sidewalks, preventive medicine...all this is amazing.

NOAM CHOMSKY

The week I was there, I got to Xi'an for a day, but most of the time I was in Beijing. I traveled around the city a fair amount and I didn't see the kind of miserable poverty that immediately strikes you whenever you go to a Third World country, and even if you walk through downtown Boston. I presume it's somewhere, but I was not seeing it.

ANDRE VLTCHEK

There is not much of it, that's the whole thing. It's another hidden secret. My best friend in China, Yuan Sheng, is a concert pianist. Whenever I go there, we just jump in his car after a concert and drive through China, both of us discovering the country. Sometimes we go for 5,000 kilometers, all around

China. We never have a concrete plan; it is all very spontaneous. Once in a while, we just stick our finger on some spot on the map, and go.

What is really striking is that even in the villages now there are solar panels on the roofs; there are good roads; there are good railroads; there are medical posts. Again I am not saying it's perfect, but having lived around the world, I can compare it to countries with the same development level as China, in terms of GDP per capita and HDI, and nobody could convince me, after what I saw, that China is a capitalist country. I think it is exactly what the government calls it: "Chinese-style socialism," a very unique model, with central planning, and the majority of the economy in government's hands. I don't want to say there are no disparities between, let's say, Beijing or Shanghai and the villages in the west of China, but what I am saying is that even the villages now have many sound ecological projects, they have decent medical post, they have decent education, and the rural areas are increasingly linked to the rest of China. And the government is shifting funding from the cities to the countryside.

There are huge medical reforms going on all over China right now. Many people who go to China with an open mind are very impressed. I am also very encouraged by the optimism of their people.

NOAM CHOMSKY

Yes, that's what really struck me. I mostly saw students, but they are very excited about the future, the opportunities. They don't like the constraints, but the sense of optimism and enthusiasm was really infectious.

ANDRE VLTCHEK

The other day I was sitting in Beijing with my friends, somewhere in the city, and we were talking about the opposition, because if you read the *Herald Tribune* you would think that all of China is up in arms against the government. And my friends said to me something very interesting. They said that of course there are plenty of protests all over China, but just look very carefully at the protesters; look what many of the people are holding in their hands. They are actually holding the flags of the Communist Party of China. So it is not that when they protest they want a Western-style capitalist economic system, or a Western-style political system. They want Communism, or socialism—the system that would represent the majority of the people. They want more socialism instead of more pro-market reforms. But if they succeed, it would be a Chinese blend of socialism.

In the West, whether China is socialist or not, it is judged by a Western interpretation of what socialism is. But this biggest country on earth has its own measures, standards and ideas. The way China is being judged in Europe and the U.S. is arrogant, thoroughly patronizing.

6

Latin America

ANDRE VLTCHEK

I would like to turn now to Latin America. The recent victories of progressive governments there are mind-blowing. One fascist, pro-Western government after another had fallen. Venezuela is leading the way, but there are also countries like Ecuador and Bolivia, the poorest and the most indigenous nation in South America. The continent is rising. And to some degree, Uruguay, Argentina, and Brazil are caring more about their own people than about international banks and companies. It is a total reverse of the norm just two decades ago. There is also an increasing sense of solidarity.

Of course the progress has its serious setbacks. The left lost Honduras and Paraguay—in two coups orchestrated by the West. And there is, of course, the entire terrible legacy of the Monroe Doctrine that is haunting the continent.

Not so long ago I visited El Salvador. Now El Salvador has a progressive government, but it seems to have its hands tied because the U.S. is unwilling to take any responsibility for the past. No reparations are paid.

There is still terrible violence as a result of the U.S. supporting the death squads that used to fight the left-wing guerrillas during the war. The violence in Salvador today is appalling, despicable. Even I was shot at; my car was shot at as I was filming. Then

I went to a village to interview the only survivor of the most horrible massacre in which 30 people were killed during the war; one family totally wiped out. As I was talking to him, I was warned that it's time to leave, because the sun was setting and *Maras*, the gangs, are taking over the area. I was lucky to get out of the place alive. The last thing that this gentleman who survived the massacre told me was that this is all a continuation of the culture of violence that was begun by the United States during the civil war.

So while there are some progressive forces and even progressive governments in many Latin American countries, they have to deal with the legacy of decades of the most despicable violence. I saw the same situation in Panama, in the city of Colón; and hardly anyone writes about it. I thought that Colón was going to be just another problematic town. I couldn't find any information except two or three articles; one of them claiming that it is the most dangerous city in the Western hemisphere. I went there and sure enough, it's an absolute wreckage of a city.

10   War-wrecked Colón, Panama, almost a quarter of a century after the U.S. invasion. (Copyright Andre Vltchek)

The destruction screams at you, with ten-year-old prostitutes on the sidewalks and American military ships docked at the cruise ship port… ships that are actually not supposed to be there because they were ordered to leave a long time ago under the treaties between Panama and the U.S. Like they were supposed to leave the Philippines, but are still there under the cover of the "war on terror." The Philippines, Panama—the same.

So there, a few miles from the iconic Panama Canal, there is the second largest city in the country, a country with, on paper, a fairly high level of development (the United Nations' human development index, HDI, is 58) but all you can see is absolutely destroyed urban sprawl. You see only a skeleton of the city.

NOAM CHOMSKY

You can't find out about the U.S. invasion of Panama. It looked to me worse than the Iraqi invasion of Kuwait. More people were killed. According to Human Rights Watch, in Kuwait the Iraqis killed a few hundred people, but in Panama it might have been a couple of thousand. CODEHUCA, the civil rights human rights group, estimates a couple of thousand.

ANDRE VLTCHEK

Three and a half thousand is increasingly the number that is agreed on. What is really interesting is how they cleaned up the whole evidence. Colón is one of the most devastated cities on earth for many different reasons: because of the gangs, because of the poverty, mismanagement. But what they managed to do was to clean up all the evidence related to the bombings and U.S. invasion. During the invasion, they even bombed the condominium, the tallest building in the city. I photographed it and there could be no mistake, they had to be aware that it was a civilian target.

The invasion was obviously very brutal, but there are some things that are extremely difficult to prove, in Panama, as in El Salvador or Nicaragua or Honduras. Things were covered up. One would have to spend several years to investigate the impact on each country. Not many journalists and scientists can do that.

In the case of Panama, the spite for its people goes back to the time of the construction of the Panama Canal. Apparently the place where I was staying, right near Colón, which is called the Rainbow City, was where the racial segregation was the most common. I was told that by my Panamanian colleagues, who didn't experience it themselves, but their grandparents and their parents told them all about the bad old days when the U.S. construction crews arrived in Colón. The segregation and racism they brought with them were thoroughly shocking to the Panamanians. And so the country that has been claiming that it is defending principals and ideals of equality, freedom, and liberty and human rights, comes to Central America, starts building the canal and segregates the local population, and builds different shops and supermarkets and housing for different races.

NOAM CHOMSKY

It happens all over the world. It's one of the reasons NGOs are such a dubious contribution: not all, of course, but many. In Haiti, in East Timor, everywhere. They live totally differently, differently to local people. They are eating in fancy restaurants, driving nice cars, while people are starving.

ANDRE VLTCHEK

This approach, "us and them," also explains the spite with which the European and U.S. invaders have been treating local population during the incursions and annexations.

NOAM CHOMSKY

There were a lot of things that had to be really suppressed. The criminal charges against Manuel Noriega were primarily from the period when he was a CIA asset. They turned against him because he wasn't cooperating with their support for the Contras in Nicaragua, so he became an enemy, but the charges were for the early 1980s when the U.S. was praising the amazing free elections he won in 1984—with murder and fraud, and secret funding from Washington to assure that Noriega's candidate would win. Secretary of State George Shultz flew down to praise Noriega for "initiating the process of democracy"—not such a strange comment in light of the Reaganite concept of "promoting democracy." Passed virtually without comment here in the mainstream. It was not that different with Saddam Hussein.

ANDRE VLTCHEK

How much is known now in the United States about these two involvements that the U.S. had—in Panama and also in El Salvador—that had such a devastating impact on both societies?

NOAM CHOMSKY

Well, essentially nothing. On the 25th anniversary of Óscar Romero's assassination, here in Boston—but it was similar elsewhere—there was one commemoration that I know of. It was in a church in a poor neighborhood in Jamaica Plain, a mostly Latino/Black area. One of the people who spoke—I was pleased to be invited to join her—was the widow of Herbert Anaya, the human rights activist who was murdered by security forces. But that was it: nothing else in the Boston area.

On the 20th anniversary of the assassination of the Jesuits, there was one commemoration at Boston College, a pretty conservative Jesuit college. I was one of the speakers here too. One of the other speakers was Jan Sobrino, the sole survivor of the Jesuit massacre in 1989. He gave quite a moving speech in which he emphasized that we should really be mourning the housekeeper and her daughter who were killed so there wouldn't be any witnesses. He said they are the symbols of the suffering of the people in El Salvador and throughout the world. And that's what we should be concerned with. A fair number of people came from the college, but outside of that I don't think there was anything.

Actually I talked about it in Europe on the anniversary too, where there was scarcely a whisper of recognition. One difference was in Ireland. In Ireland they understood; there were close connections—a lot of Irish priests were in Central America and in fact one of the main sources of information about what was going on at the time was the Irish press because they were getting information back from priests on the ground.

ANDRE VLTCHEK

There were some progressive priests.

NOAM CHOMSKY

Well, yes, but they weren't all particularly progressive; they were just caught like Romero himself. He was conservative, but he became deeply engaged when his own priests started to be murdered. He was a serious, honest person. And these priests were like that too.

There is a Roman Catholic order of nuns active in Nicaragua, the Religious of the Assumption. I was told they were actually living under a death threat from the former government. When I was there my friend César Jerez took me out to one of their convents next to an extremely poor village. The Mother Superior was going around to huts to convince reluctant peasants to be vaccinated. The nuns had succeeded in getting the villagers, apparently for the first time, to cooperate on building a well. The well was on a hill. An ox climbed up the hill with a rope around its neck, pulling a bucket which went down to the well. And the ox came down the hill and they had easy access to freshwater for the first time. But what was striking was that they were working together.

It reminded me of William Hinton's description of what happened in the early days of the Chinese revolution. One of the striking things was trying to get peasants who were used to being in conflict with each other (like you move a rock two inches so you can have a little more land from the guy next to you) to realize that they can cooperate and do things together. That's what the nuns of the convent were doing. They were not progressive, but they are just human. A lot of church activities were like that.

It was the same with support groups here. There were quite substantial Central American support groups in the 1980s, but you'd find more of them in rural communities in Kansas or Arizona than you would in the main cities. They were largely church-based groups; a lot of these were evangelical. And in fact they were the ones who persisted after the U.S. destroyed

Nicaragua. There were few groups who continued their solidarity work after Violeta Chamorro was elected president in 1990. Most of the activist groups pulled out, but not these groups; they were really dedicated. I was impressed with them.

ANDRE VLTCHEK

To come back to Panama, do you think that one of the reasons the U.S. decided to invade was because Noriega was advocating and conducting relatively decent social policies inside his country? Of course we could never call him a leftist, but again, as with the case of Saddam Hussein or the case of Gaddafi in Libya, we're talking about a country that was implementing at least a skeleton of social systems in a part of the world known for its social ruthlessness.

NOAM CHOMSKY

Maybe, but that would not have been enough because he was not doing that much. I think he just turned. In the early 1980s he was working with the United States, he was basically a CIA asset helping support the Contras and so on. The U.S. counted on him—Panama was considered a base of U.S. power. But by the late 1980s Noriega was becoming more independent, and so then the attacks began: "narcotrafficker," "terrorist," "torturer." And when he was finally tried, the charges were mostly from the period when he was a U.S. favorite. I think the reason for the U.S. invasion was mainly Noriega's growing independence.

ANDRE VLTCHEK

There is also the Panama Canal there, one of the most strategic waterways in the world.

NOAM CHOMSKY

The canal, of course. The worst country in the Western hemisphere right now is Honduras, where the violence is totally out of control. There are two countries in the last decade in the Western hemisphere where the United States has been involved in successful military coups. They tried one in Venezuela, but it failed. The next one was Haiti, where the U.S. and France, the traditional torturers of Haiti, basically invaded and kidnapped a president they didn't like, and sent him off to Central Africa, and still won't let his party run in elections in Haiti.

Third was Honduras, under the Obama administration. There was a military coup in Honduras, and the president was kidnapped. There were some ritual criticisms, but pretty soon the U.S. broke from almost the entire continent, and even Europe, and supported the fraudulent election carried out by the new military dictatorship and the atrocities that are going on right now. Like the killing of human rights activists, labor activists, extensive killings. The country is being torn to shreds. But it's the last solid U.S. base in the hemisphere, it contains a major U.S. air base and it supports U.S. investment, so the atrocities are accepted....

Actually what is happening in El Salvador right now is a perfect example of the kind of indirect destruction that you were mentioning before. So right now the current government of Salvador has tried to institute some rule of law to protect parts of the country from environmental disaster. But that was going to take away potential profits, from gold mining. Multinational gold mining is the most destructive mining there is. The multinational brought a case against El Salvador under World Trade Organization rules, charging El Salvador with taking their profits illegally by trying to protect parts of the environment from destruction by gold mining. It went to the courts, and the multinational won.

The World Trade Organization rules, the international rules, are set up to permit multinational corporations to sue governments for infringing their potential profits when they destroy a country. Now, that doesn't look like going out and killing people with a machete, but it is. And that's built into the highly praised rules of the neoliberal system; lauded by international authorities, by economists and so on. It's not the first such case, but it is happening right at the moment. And in fact mining throughout the world is just a horrendous disaster. I mean, half of India is at war over it. In Colombia there are struggles against it. In Australia the indigenous population is trying to block the destruction of what's left of the country for them. Just everywhere.

ANDRE VLTCHEK

There is increasing cooperation amongst the left-wing states of Latin America. One of the most significant cases was when the rich and the predominantly white province of Santa Cruz in Bolivia threatened to declare independence several years ago. It was clear that the West was involved, that business interests were involved and so were the local elites. It was the way to hurt, to destroy Bolivia and the left-wing reforms of President Evo Morales. Brazil basically said that they were going to send in the army to protect the integrity of their neighboring country. In a way, Brazil saved Bolivia and its socialist government. Again, this would have been unimaginable just two decades ago.

NOAM CHOMSKY

It was quite interesting, I think, that UNASUR, the Union of the South American Republics, which has just been formed, actually took a pretty strong position against it. The first thing they did was to support the president. This was barely mentioned here but that was quite also significant.

The Summit of the Americas in Cartagena, Colombia, was also quite interesting. The only thing that was reported here was that the secret service went out with prostitutes, but what actually happened was quite significant. There were two main issues. One was the admission of Cuba. The U.S. refused, but the rest of the continent insisted on it, Canada aside. They finally agreed to put it off this time, but it's very unlikely that it'll happen again if there is ever another hemispheric meeting. So Cuba would be admitted and the United States—and Canada if it continues to follow the U.S. line—would be excluded.

11   Police next to a mural declaring "Freedom" in Bogotá, Colombia. (Copyright Andre Vltchek)

The other issue is the drug war. Overwhelmingly on the continent they want to call it to an end. Colombian legislators have gone so far as to introduce legislation to decriminalize all drugs and there are similar moves elsewhere. They all understand perfectly well that the drug war just serves U.S. interests. The demand for drugs is here, the supply of arms is here (most of the arms in Mexico that are used for slaughtering people are coming from Arizona and Texas), but it is destroying the people of Central and South America. And despite everything, the use of drugs stays the same or worsens. And so the countries of Latin America want to get out of this U.S. war that is destroying their societies. The U.S. and Canada were almost completely isolated in their opposition.

Well, here you have a hemispheric conference with two major issues on which the hemisphere is pretty united, and the U.S. and Canada are excluded: that's a major change in world affairs. This used to be what they called the backyard, the plaything of the U.S.: "We do what we like there." Now it is moving towards serious independence. In fact there has already, about a year ago, been a new organization formed in Venezuela, the CELAC (Caribbean and Latin American countries), which formally excludes the U.S. and Canada. It's the hemisphere minus the U.S. and Canada—that would have been unthinkable ten years ago.

ANDRE VLTCHEK

It would have been unthinkable, I agree. And let's not forget that narcotics are coming from Colombia, which is actually one of the last allies of the United States in South America. It has the only right-wing government—except the one in Chile, which will not last for long.

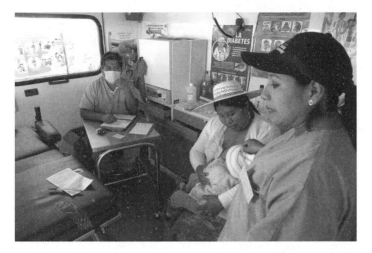

12   Free mobile clinics in Cochabamba, Bolivia.
(Copyright Andre Vltchek)

I was in Bolivia very recently and was very impressed. I spent the entire day on the main square of Cochabamba, observing the doctors—both Bolivian doctors and those from Cuba. There was such tremendous segregation in Bolivia before, and it was overwhelming to now see mobile clinics and white doctors serving indigenous people; mothers with their children coming in thousands to register their babies, because most of them were born out of wedlock. For decades they had no rights, but now the government is asking them to register so they can get social benefits. Dozens of nutritionists were at work, informing people about a healthy diet based on what the country and the villages have been producing. The entire city centre had been converted to one huge social-medical post. The government of Bolivia was actually collecting people from the villages, encouraging them to come to the city and to register and to get free health care.

As I was leaving the city for La Paz, I felt very emotional, and very hopeful.

Venezuela is another country that I find very impressive in so many different ways. Two years ago, I visited Venezuela and worked in the anti-Chavez city of Maracaibo. I wanted to see how they—the reactionaries—think. I also went to Mérida, to Ciudad Bolivar, to Caracas of course, and to Canaima, the indigenous land in the middle of the jungle. I remember sitting in a *porpuesto*, one of those huge shared taxis, approaching Ciudad Bolivar, packed with opposition guys. I wanted to hear what they had to say, so I kept asking questions. They were actually friendly to me, probably because they knew I was holding a U.S. passport.

One of them said: "Oh, you come from abroad; it's easy for you to support Chavez. Eventually you will get out and at home you have democracy. We don't have any democracy here." I remember telling them: "Look, to compare democracy in your country and in my country is like sitting in the same car on this same road... but in the U.S. if I'd vote it would be between the choice of driving in the same direction, but in the left or right lane. But when you vote here; for Chavez or against Chavez, it is like going forward or going backward." They didn't want to hear it, but they enjoyed the metaphor; they were all laughing. But that's how I think it really is.

In Chile they had 20 years of the Concertación government. It was not very left wing, but it was such a sharp departure from what they had during the Pinochet dictatorship. The situation all over Latin America also influenced Chile, moved it to the left. And then Michelle Bachelet Jeria was elected president: a socialist and a woman who was tortured during the dictatorship, whose father was murdered. But even though she was enormously popular she couldn't run for a second term because the constitution forbids a second consecutive term, and so a conservative businessman, Sebastián Piñera, came to power. But Chile remains a social democratic country. Not really socialist at the moment, but social democratic. There is nothing the government can do to stop or reverse the process in just four years. The people are now demanding free education and free medical care, there is optimism and hope, and there is struggle. Chile matters a lot, as it is the most advanced country in Latin America, the one with great socialist traditions, and with enormous progressive culture.

After Pinochet was forced to resign, the country was totally in private hands. There began a slow process of reversing the trend inherited from long years of dictatorship. The government began building a so-called "catastrophic illness" medical plan—the idea was that the bill for the most devastating illnesses would be covered by the state. At first, only four or five conditions were covered—almost nothing. But now it is more than a hundred. Fully socialized medical care could not be afforded right from the beginning, so they kept adding medical conditions and illnesses to the list of catastrophic illnesses, one by one.

Now Chile has very good public hospitals. Things are not perfect: you still have to register, you have to pay something for the treatment—sometimes just a token amount, sometimes a serious amount of money. And of course Chile has a few problems with education, as we know, which is not free at university level, unlike in Mexico and Argentina. But the Chilean people are fighting for fully free medical care now, together with totally free education, and as one of the richest countries in the Western hemisphere they may achieve both goals, soon.

NOAM CHOMSKY

The first time I went to Chile was a couple of year after the fall of Pinochet. It must have been around 1995. I was in Concepción: it's a beautiful city, a lovely place. My friends there told me that they were still afraid to talk to their own friends. This was a couple of years into the Concertación period and there remained an atmosphere of fear. Nobody knew who was an informer. And I noticed that when I was talking to journalists, if there were soldiers standing by, they'd stop talking. Actually once, I was walking across a large university campus with friends and we passed by a big empty building. I asked how come it was empty, and they explained that it was supposed to be a dormitory, but the military had said they couldn't have students on campus. So therefore it's empty. And what struck me about it was that they didn't think that they could do anything about it.

ANDRE VLTCHEK

I first went to Chile maybe two or three years after the dictatorship had fallen and I ended up living there for about three years. First it was terrible, chilling, as you described. People were scared. Almost all doormen in Santiago were snitches. But very soon you could see how the society was beginning to change, regenerate.

My best friend in Chile is an architect and photographer, Alejandro Wagner. I remember how during this time we would drive together in my car and when he saw the police he would just get so scared, even if our car had a foreign license plate. But he was a Chilean, and so he was still afraid to be stopped.

These days there are open political demonstrations in Santiago and the police just stand by. Periodically the students clash with the police, but now both sides get injured, not just the demonstrators. One could almost call it an equal fight. But what a change, what a departure from the past!

NOAM CHOMSKY

I saw something like that in Nicaragua. One of my closest friends in Nicaragua during the 1980s was César Jérez, who was the rector of the University of Central America. He was a Guatemalan and very high up in the Jesuit order. He had to flee Guatemala when they said they were going to murder all the Jesuits. He fled to El Salvador where he was quite close to Óscar Romero. Romero was almost a peasant, and César became a kind of house intellectual for him. Romero wrote a letter to President Jimmy Carter, pleading with him not to send any military aid to the junta because they were just using it to destroy people's elementary human rights—it was César who actually wrote it.

The day after Carter would have got the letter, César received a call from the Vatican ordering him to come back to Rome. So plainly the Carter administration was watching. They knew he was the guilty party, and may have wanted the authorities to silence this troublesome priest. Back in Rome he met the head of the Jesuit order, who asked him what he was up to. Then he had an audience with the Pope. The Pope was non-committal; he didn't say "no", but he didn't say "yes." So César took that as a go-ahead. He returned to El Salvador and two days later Romero was murdered.

So César fled to Nicaragua, which was like Paris in the 1930s—the place to which people fled for safety from the murderous U.S.-backed regimes. There he became the rector of the university; the leading Jesuit figure there. I was once walking with him through the streets of Managua and we were stopped by police for some minor matter, and he preferred to be friendly—he talked to the police officer and later said to me: "This is the only country in Central America where you don't have to be afraid of the police. If they stop you, you just talk to them." If it was anywhere else you would be terrified.

ANDRE VLTCHEK

When I visited recently, I have to say that there was such an absolutely relaxed, pleasant, and comfortable feeling about Nicaragua, despite the legacy of the Arnoldo Alemán regime. It feels like a very noble society. There are statues of poets everywhere and the poems are literally hanging from the trees in the parks and engraved on the benches. People are much more literate than elsewhere in the region, compared to El Salvador or Panama.

13   The remains of a ship called *Hope* sunk by U.S.-backed Contras, Nicaragua. (Copyright Andre Vltchek)

NOAM CHOMSKY

In the 1990s I had a daughter living there, and a family there, but it was pretty depressing to visit. You got a sense of hopelessness—it had been so exciting in the 1980s; people were enthusiastic, they thought they were going to achieve something, but by the late '80s it was already a different story. People were depressed: they couldn't fight the United States. Only a few people thought that the left would lose the election in 1990; it was mainly out of fear that they did. But in the 1990s, what I could see looked like a devastated society. Men getting drunk; their wives coming out in the morning pulling them off the streets; the women doing all the things you see in really destroyed societies.

Just to give you one example, my daughter lived in what counted as a middle-class community. It was near some horrible slums, but they had better roofs, a concrete floor, electricity a couple hours a day, water overnight only (she collected it). There was a playground nearby, but it's a tropical climate so the playground equipment was rusting and the kids couldn't use it. Half the men in the neighborhood were welders, or carpenters, or something similar, but there was so little community spirit left that they wouldn't even go out on an afternoon and fix up the playground equipment for their own children. I felt that if it had been ten years earlier, then some neighborhood committee would have done it. But there was a sense of: "We tried hard, we were beaten back, we can't do anything."

ANDRE VLTCHEK

I remember that. Some ten years ago, when I lived in Costa Rica, I would drive to Nicaragua, to talk to old Sandinista, to see what was happening to them. I spoke to Edén Pastora, to Daniel

Ortega (who since 2007 has again been president of Nicaragua), but it was hopeless. Before the elections, the U.S. Ambassador would almost openly spread the message that if the Sandinistas won, then the campaign of terror would be re-launched. It was a mafia approach: "You do as we say or we break your leg." So people voted right-wing out of fear.

In a way you also see this spirit in places like South and Southeast Asia, where people are broken, from Indonesia, to the Philippines, to India. You see it in Africa. You can try only so much. If you try and try, only to be beaten back, then you lose hope and strength to fight. Fortunately, things have changed so greatly all over Latin America!

Some five or six years ago I met the great Uruguayan writer Eduardo Galeano, in his favorite café, Brasileiro in Montevideo. We talked for many hours. He told me one thing that I often remember: "The worst thing you can do to the poor is to take away their hope." He said to take away hope from the poor is worse than murdering someone. Because once you are dead, you are dead. But hope is often all that the poor have, all that sustains them. He explained: "That's why I am saying to all my people here on the continent, 'Comrades, don't play with people's hope! Keep your promises.'" I believe that for the first time, there are several Latin American leaders doing all they can in order not to betray the hopes of their people.

7

The Middle East
and the Arab Spring

ANDRE VLTCHEK

One thing we must talk about is the Middle East. Perhaps we could start with the glorified prime minister Winston Churchill and his statements about the Middle East, and his involvement in the region right after World War II.

NOAM CHOMSKY

I thought of him as hideous, a racist, but so was the British ruling class. The British pioneered the use of aircraft against villagers. Churchill himself favored poisoned gas: not the most lethal kind, just enough to strike "lively terror" into the hearts of "uncivilized tribesmen." After World War I, such things happened, the Royal Air Force was used to bomb Kurdish, Afghan and Iraqi civilians. Iraq was sort of created by the British in their own interests. There was a rebellion, a Shi'ite rebellion, and they crushed it with aircraft. There was a disarmament conference to bar the use of aircraft against civilians and the British succeeded in killing it. If you take a look at Lloyd George's diary at that time, he praised

14   Slums encircling Lima, Peru. (Copyright Andre Vltchek)

this. He said it's a very good thing to do because we have to "reserve the right to bomb niggers."

And so yes, Churchill was horrible, but so was everybody else with very few exceptions. But the racism was incredible—and it goes on. The British were gradually losing their control over the Middle East, because Britain was becoming much weaker after World War I and Britain; although it was nothing like it had been before, it did remain the major imperial power in the world, including over the Middle East, until World War II. But even through World War II, there was a kind of mini war going on between the United States and Britain over Saudi Arabia. American oil companies, in the late 1930s, had discovered oil in Saudi Arabia. They realized it was pretty big, although they didn't know quite how big. The British were there too and during World War II there was a conflict over who was going to take control of it. The British tried; they had assets, background and people.

The U.S. was worried about it. One high-up American diplomat warned that the British were trying to "diddle [U.S. companies] out of the concession," to take over U.S. concessions in Saudi Arabia. Well, the way to stop this was for Roosevelt to issue a presidential edict determining that Saudi Arabia was a democratic ally in the forefront of the battle against Nazism, or some such wording. That enabled them to get Lend Lease aid, so they were able to buy off the ruling family with their thanks for being a leading democracy and fighting the war against the Nazis. The war ended with the United States in control. And by the end of World War II, when the U.S. was dividing up the world, they kicked out the French on very similar grounds. The argument was that the French were fascist collaborators, because of Vichy; they had lost their rights by being conquered. The U.S. performed some legal trickery at the State Department. The British were allowed to stay, but as a junior partner.

When you get to the Iranian coup, in 1953, the British tried to carry it off, but they couldn't do it. They needed U.S. backing. They got Eisenhower's support and basically with a U.S. lead they were able to overthrow the government. But one condition was that the American oil companies had to take 40 percent of the British concession. Rather interestingly the American companies didn't want this, because there was a lot of oil, and oil from Saudi Arabia was cheaper. They made more profit from Saudi Arabia, and they knew that they would irritate the Saudis if they shifted operations to Iran, so they refused. The government ordered them to take the concession, and the Eisenhower administration threatened them with anti-trust suits unless they followed orders and took over 40 percent of the Iranian concession. This was one of the rare cases in which state power overrules concentrated corporate power because the state authorities are taking a longer term view of things, not just the question of profits tomorrow.

Actually, Cuba is like that. American corporations have for years wanted to enter into normal relations with Cuba: huge sectors of the corporate system—agribusiness, energy, pharmaceuticals—these are not small actors. But the government won't let them, because America has to punish Cuba for what Washington called "successful defiance" of U.S. policy going back 150 years, to the Monroe Doctrine of 1823. The Monroe Doctrine announced that America was going to take over the hemisphere. So the Cubans have to be punished for their successful defiance, while the American population, the large majority, is in favor of normalization. OK, they are disregarded, but that's normal. What's more striking is that major sectors of economic power are overruled, as in the case of Iran in 1953.

I think this is true of Iran now, as well. Since it is a contemporary event, we do not actually have records, but I bet when they come out, they are going to show that the energy corporations would like to get back into Iran. They don't want to leave it to the Chinese, but the government's going to forbid them to do so because we have to punish Iran.

Anyhow, going back to the Middle East after World War II. The British role in Iran was reduced and the U.S. began to take over. In Iraq in 1958, there was a so-called independent government, but it was basically British-run, and it was overthrown in a military coup. A couple years later the U.S. was able to engineer a coup that overthrew the Nasser-type nationalist government, and that's where Saddam Hussein comes in. The CIA handed the new Ba'athist government a long list of Communists, radicals, and teachers, and then they all got assassinated. Then you come to the present; the U.S. expects to run Iraq. In Saudi Arabia, the British were the junior partner. Finally the British pulled out, and left it to the United States.

ANDRE VLTCHEK

Of course Saudi Arabia is a tremendously destabilizing force in the world and its influence spreads from Bahrain to Indonesia. In Bahrain there is the fear that the country may be annexed by Saudi Arabia. The Saudi army is in and out of Bahrain.

NOAM CHOMSKY

The Saudis are pouring money all over the place to sponsor the most extreme forms of radical Islamism—Wahabbism—in Madrasas, in Pakistan, pouring money into Egypt to support the Salafis, all extreme Islamic elements. The United States is happy with that; it doesn't try to prevent them.

The idea that the U.S. is opposed to radical Islam is ludicrous. The most extreme fundamentalist Islamic state in the world is Saudi Arabia, which is the U.S.'s favorite. Britain also has consistently supported radical Islam. The reason was to oppose secular nationalism. U.S. relations with Israel reached their current close state in 1967 because Israel performed the huge service of smashing secular nationalism and defending radical Islam.

A British diplomatic historian, Mark Curtis, wrote a very good book a few years ago called *Secret Affairs: British Collusion with Radical Islam*. Curtis went through the British records on Islam. It turns out the British had consistently supported radical Islamist elements, pretty much what the U.S. has been doing. They may not have liked it but they prefer them to the secular nationalists.

Secular nationalists threatened them—they threatened to take over the resources and use them for domestic development and that's the worst sin; so we support radical Islamists.

ANDRE VLTCHEK

U.S. support for the Mujahedeen in Afghanistan is well documented, but what is not so well known is that almost all radical Islam in Southeast Asia is somehow connected to that war in Afghanistan. That's actually where the Southeast Asian radical Islamic cadres got radicalized and indoctrinated, on the battlefields of Afghanistan. There they were fighting on behalf of the West; they were paid by Western money and armed by Washington and London.

NOAM CHOMSKY

It is all over; in Libya, Algeria....

ANDRE VLTCHEK

The Arab Spring itself is a very complex, controversial subject. How do you see the developments in Egypt and Tunisia?

NOAM CHOMSKY

First of all, what happened was of really historic significance. There have been plenty of problems, but what has already been achieved is quite significant. Quite naturally the Islamist forces have essentially taken over the parliamentary system. They have been organized for decades. They are strongly supported by a flood of money from Saudi Arabia, which has the most reactionary form of Islamism existing anywhere. And the U.S.,

Britain, and France are quite willing to tolerate the Islamist Muslim Brotherhood because they are basically neoliberal.

In Tunisia a rather moderate Islamist party, Ennahda, essentially took over. In Egypt it is still work in process. But what is quite striking is that these two countries—Egypt and Tunisia—where there was the most progress, are the two countries which had a powerful militant labor movement, which had been struggling for years to gain labor rights. In Egypt the Tahrir Square demonstrations were led by, initiated by, what is called the April 6 Movement, a movement of young professionals. Why April 6? Well, because on April 6, 2008 there were major labor protests organized at the Mahalla industrial conglomerate with supporting activities elsewhere which were crushed by the dictatorship. A group of young professionals joined together to continue the struggle under that name and they sparked the January 2011 uprisings, the Egypt Arab Spring.

15   Protest in front of the Presidential Palace, Cairo, February 2013.
(Copyright Andre Vltchek)

One of the real achievements of the Arab Spring in Egypt has been to reduce, maybe eliminate, constraints on labor organizing. So for the first time they have been able to organize their independent unions, something that was never possible before, and maybe move towards more independence. There were cases of workers taking over factories and that is all very positive. But it has yet to manifest itself within the parliamentary system.

The other achievement in both Egypt and Tunisia is an extreme relaxation of the constraints of freedom of speech and expression. So now the press and media are quite free and open; there is free and open discussion. All these are very important developments. The military is still in place, more so in Egypt than in Tunisia, but I suspect we will see that this ferment which has been created will go on to something further. It's very much at an early stage.

As far as the U.S. and the West are concerned, it would be almost intolerable to allow functioning democracy in this region. And if anyone wants to know the reason, it's very easy to find out. All you have to do is look at the polls right before the Arab Spring broke out. In late 2010, on the eve of the Arab Spring, there were polls of opinion in the Arab world, in particular in Egypt, undertaken by the main Western polling agencies, and there have been other polls since with generally similar results. So for example, in Egypt, the most important country, about 80 percent of the population, maybe higher, regard the United States and Israel as the main threats they face. And maybe 10 percent regard Iran as a threat. In fact, opposition to U.S. policy is so strong that a considerable majority thought the region would be better off if Iran had nuclear weapons to offset U.S. power and Israeli power as the client of the U.S. Results were partially similar across the Arab world.

Well, if you have a functioning democracy, then popular opinions would have some influence on policy. And so it's pretty obvious that London, Paris, and Washington are not going to allow this to happen if they can help it. They have to do whatever they can to undermine the democratic elements of the Arab Spring, which in fact is what they have been doing. And that is quite consistent with past practice, not just in this region. In the countries that they care about most, the oil dictatorships, there has been essentially nothing, no change. Their uprisings were quickly repressed. In Bahrain, Saudi Arabia brought in a military force, which enabled the king to crush the protests pretty violently, by breaking into the hospitals, by torture and so on. There were a couple of words of criticism from the West but not a lot. And, most significantly, in eastern Saudi Arabia there is a Shi'ite population, which has been pretty harshly repressed. That is the area where most of the oil is, so it's very sensitive.

In Egypt and Tunisia, the U.S. and its allies followed the traditional game plan, which has been used over and over again, where some favored dictator can't hold on any longer—maybe the army turns against him—like Somoza, Marcos, Duvalier, Suharto, Mobutu, and others. Support him to the last moment and when it becomes impossible send him off somewhere and try to restore the old order, and of course talk about how much you love democracy. It's routine. It takes real genius not to see it.

Actually there is also an interesting case in Eastern Europe: Ceaușescu, who was the worst of the Communist dictators but the darling of the West. Reagan and Thatcher loved him. Until the last minute they were supporting him and when it became impossible (he was in fact overthrown and killed) then the routine plan was reintroduced. That's exactly what they have been doing in Egypt and Tunisia. Somehow it can't be seen. It's another example of the internal colonization. No matter how many times it happens you can't see it. The only thing that we can see is our love of democracy.

ANDRE VLTCHEK

One thing that I feel is missing in what's called the Arab Spring is solidarity between the Arab countries. Their rebellion appears to be very fragmented. Even the popular and very positive rebellions appeared to be atomized.

NOAM CHOMSKY

I think the Arab Spring is still at an incipient stage. It has only been in roughly the last decade that Latin America has, for the first time since the conquistadores, moved towards integration and independence. It also began dealing with some of its internal social problems, which are horrendous. These are developments of really historic significance, and if the Arab Spring moves in the same direction, which it still may, it will change the nature of world order significantly, which is why the West is doing everything to try to stop this.

My suspicion is that the government will soon lose all their credibility, they will not be able to deal with the fundamental problems that the uprisings were about: the neo-liberal policies and their effects. They will just reinstitute them. I think that would continue the disaster and, with the experience of the last few years and the real although limited successes, probably lead to a new uprising.

ANDRE VLTCHEK

In the Western attempt to pass the UN resolution against Syria, Russia and China opposed them. This was a clear signal that both powers—China and Russia—are unwilling to take orders from the West, and are ready to cooperate in opposing Western imperialism. It was a very important development, but one that was interpreted in the most vitriolic way in the mainstream media.

NOAM CHOMSKY

It was not just Russia and China: all the BRICS countries— Brazil, Russia, India, China, South Africa—opposed military intervention. It's more convenient to blame it on Russia and China, because they are the official enemies so it fits the propaganda image. My guess is that if we had internal records, we'd find that the U.S. State Department and Obama are very happy that Russia and China vetoed the UN resolution. That gives a pretext for not doing anything, claiming, "gosh, we'd love to intervene and help them out but what can we do?"

16   Training camp for Syrian "opposition," near Hatay, Turkey.
(Copyright Andre Vltchek)

I mean, if the U.S. wanted to intervene, they wouldn't care one way or another what the Security Council decides. It totally disregards it, over and over again, but this gives a convenient pretext. It's pretty clear that they don't want to become directly involved, because they are not so clear who they are supporting, what the outcomes would be. Whatever you think about Assad in the past, he pretty well conformed to U.S. and Israeli interests; kept things stable and so on. As for the business classes, some post-Assad regime could be much less amenable to their interests. So they are trying to stay out and this way they can blame Russia and China, keep quiet about the role of the BRICS, and not mention the fact that if we wanted to do anything, we wouldn't care either way.

ANDRE VLTCHEK

There are other Latin American countries, such as Bolivia, who were opposed to the resolution. But Latin American revolutionary governments are so popular all over the world that I agree with you: the West finds it much easier to blame the resolution on two countries that it spends all its efforts on discrediting: China and Russia.

NOAM CHOMSKY

That is true on most issues, like Libya, for example. There was practically no support for the bombing outside the three traditional imperial powers: Britain, France, and the United States. The African Union was calling for negotiations and diplomacy; the BRICS countries again called for negotiations and diplomacy. The International Crisis Group, the main non-governmental agency, took a similar stand. And in Latin

America again, and the non-aligned countries, and also Turkey and Germany. There was very little support for the bombing. It's called the "international community," but that term doesn't mean anything. Support was very limited and there was a reason for that. There was a UN resolution adopted in March 2011 which called for a "no fly zone," the protection of civilians, a ceasefire and negotiations. Well, the imperial powers were not having any of that. They wanted to enter into the war and to impose their own kind of government. And the world was against it because they were concerned with the likelihood that turning it into a major war would lead to a humanitarian catastrophe, which it finally did. That's one of the reasons why nobody talks about it now; Libya became a serious wreck. The final bombings in the area around Sirte, which is the base of the largest tribe in Libya—what happened to those? There were pretty awful effects. Some observers said it reminded them of Grozny.

It is the same with Iran, in fact. With Iran, it is the United States and Europe claiming that it is the greatest danger to world peace. The non-aligned countries have been vigorously supporting Iran's rights to enrich uranium for years and the BRICS countries again won't go along. India is refusing to go along; it is increasing trade with Iran. And Turkey is increasing trade relations with Iran.

The most interesting case is the Arab world. The U.S. reported here the Arabs' support for American policy on Iran. That's a very careful reference to the dictators. You know the dictators say they support the policy, but the population doesn't. Their own populations, in repeated polls, say that while they don't like Iran, they don't regard it as a serious threat. They regard the U.S. and Israel as threats. And right before the Arab Spring, the majority in Egypt said that it would be better if Iran had nuclear weapons, though they don't like Iran and surely wouldn't want them to.

ANDRE VLTCHEK

To develop nuclear weapons—it's probably the only way for Iran to survive.

NOAM CHOMSKY

Well, for the Egyptians, right before Tahrir Square it's the way to protect them from the U.S. and Israel, their main enemies. So, again, almost no support for the attack on Iran. It is a war; it is already a war. The cyber war is a war. The sanctions are virtually a blockade, which is an act of war. It is a U.S./European act, not the worlds'. And incidentally there is virtually no discussion of the most obvious way to deal with the problem. That is to initiate steps towards a nuclear weapon-free zone in the region. There is overwhelming support for that in the world, led by Egypt for many years. The U.S. has formally been required to say that it's a good idea, but not now, because of Israel. But if you are serious about nuclear weapons in the region, it's obviously the way to go.

Meanwhile U.S. intelligence continues to insist that they know of no Iranian nuclear weapons program and that if there was one, it would take years to get anywhere. So whatever you think the threat is, it's not imminent. In fact, the most interesting question of all is: "What's the threat?" There is a lot of talk about how it is the worst threat to world peace, but what exactly is the threat? There is an authoritative answer to this that doesn't get published. U.S. intelligence and the Pentagon provide an analysis every year to Congress on the global security situation, and it is public—not that it gets reported. If you read it, they say there is no military threat: Iran has very low military expenditure even by the standards of the region. They see Iran's strategic doctrine as defensive. With regard to nuclear weapons, they say, "well if they have a nuclear weapons program, that would be part of their deterrence strategy." They want to try to deter attack by, basically, the U.S. and Israel. So the real threat is that there might be a deterrent. Also they have said they are trying to destabilize neighboring countries—Iraq and Afghanistan—which means trying to expand their influence into neighboring countries. When we invade those countries and destroy them, that's called "stability." When our enemies try to strengthen commercial, political, relations, that's called "destabilizing." So that's the threat of Iran.

ANDRE VLTCHEK

Another "threat" would probably be the fact that Iran is forging alliances with other countries that the West is trying to destroy—such as Venezuela and other left-wing Latin American nations.

NOAM CHOMSKY

Which makes it even worse, of course. But in general, the worst is "not following orders"— like in case of Cuba: if they are not following orders they have to be punished.

ANDRE VLTCHEK

But you didn't see Syria necessarily as a steppingstone for the West to Iran? The West is destabilizing Syria in a very determined fashion.

NOAM CHOMSKY

Well, the West would like it to be that, but I don't see any sign, any semi-formulated plan. They are sending support to the militias, to the so-called Free Syrian Army, but indirectly; apparently it is coming straight from Qatar and Saudi Arabia, but the U.S. is maybe orchestrating it. There doesn't seem to be any indication that they really want to intervene directly, which would be very tricky. Not only militarily difficult, but it is not clear from the Western point of view what the outcome would be. They can't occupy Syria by ground military force. They can bomb, they can always bomb, but what would that achieve?

There has been an increasing amount of interesting reports recently. The German newspaper *Frankfurter Allgemeine Zeitung* had an interesting investigation of the Hula massacre and they pointed out something that I didn't see, that the people killed were from two families, Shi'ite and Alawite. And they quoted

17   Israeli fences cutting through the Golan Heights, Syria.
(Copyright Andre Vltchek)

lots of witnesses who did not want to be identified because they were terrified, saying that it was done by Islamist thugs run by the Free Syrian Army.

ANDRE VLTCHEK

Yes, there is a lot of very powerful reporting actually coming from the area, confirming how brutal many of these people are who are called "freedom fighters" and "opposition forces" by the Western media and political establishment. Not long ago, the Russian foreign minister, Lavrov, made a potent statement actually accusing the West and Saudi Arabia of supporting those forces.

I recently travelled to the area, and what I found out is that while some camps around the Turkish city of Hatay in the southeast corner of the country, which is near the Syrian border and the city of Allepo, are truly for the refugees, others like Apaydin are military camps where NATO, of which Turkey is a member, is arming and training the Syrian militias. They cross the border to Syria, at night, and some return at dawn. The border is open only for them; even Turkish citizens can't cross there anymore. Incenlik—the major air force base outside the city of Adana—is also used as a training facility for the "Syrian opposition."

NOAM CHOMSKY

Fascinating. These are the first detailed reports I've actually seen from the scene. I sent the *Frankfurter Allgemeine Zeitung* story to Medialens, a critical media group in London, and they sent it to the *Guardian* but the *Guardian* wouldn't print it.

ANDRE VLTCHEK

It's a very "sensitive" issue. I am working with a team of Turkish reporters from Aydinlik and Ulusal television channel; quite outspoken and courageous people. They have actually been investigating the camps for a long time. They went to the camps on the Syrian border, particularly to those around the city of Hatay. And they followed the fighters who are being trained on the Turkish territory—they followed them all the way to Syria, to Damascus.

NOAM CHOMSKY

They managed to do that?

ANDRE VLTCHEK

Yes, and they have been sharing their footage as well as their still images with me. I am supplying them with my films and with my analyses from other parts of the world, and they are giving me access to their work. I find it very important, what they have been doing. They were uncovering; unveiling the true face of so-called Syrian opposition; like who they really are, who sponsors them, what are their goals. And this is again something that is very rarely covered in the West.

Turkey itself is a very interesting, a unique country. The two close allies of the United States in the Middle East, Israel and Turkey, appear to be in verbal conflict. But my friends and colleagues in Istanbul are saying that their government is not really serious in confronting Israel. Turkey is still a very close ally of the United States, which has strategic military bases on Turkish territory.

NOAM CHOMSKY

I think that under the circumstances Turkey is moving in an independent direction in many ways. For example, in 2003

Turkey refused U.S. orders to allow it to be used as a base for the war against Iraq. That was serious and the U.S. government was pretty upset by that. They threatened Turkey with sanctions. Paul Wolfowitz, then Deputy Secretary of Defense—he's supposed to be a great "democracy advocate"— lectured the Turkish military on its failure to compel the government to overrule 95 per cent of the population and follow Washington's orders. He said that Turkey must realize that their duty is to support the United States and they must apologize. This event cooled relations with Ankara.

It's true that they kept the bases in the east. In relation to Israel, part of Erdogan's turn to the East was to appear as the one international leader who took a very strong stand against the Israeli attack on Gaza over the winter of 2008/09. He also strongly condemned the attack on the Mavi Marmara, the Turkish-backed ship that was attempting to break through the Israeli naval blockade of Gaza. It was an attack in international waters by Israeli commandos wich killed nine people, mainly Turks and one American. Turkey demanded an apology. That's significant because Turkey was Israel's main ally outside the United States. Back in 1958 they both had an anti-Arab agenda, so just as Israel was closely allied with the Shah, for similar reasons they also had a very close alliance with Turkey. Your friends may be right, I don't know the details, but it's not the relation that it was, and it might break.

ANDRE VLTCHEK

There is a set of serious concerns in Turkey now. Particularly in Istanbul, it appears that most of the secular and left-wing intellectual community is horrified by the arrests that have been taking place over the last few years. Hundreds of people have disappeared; many, allegedly, have been tortured. The military establishment that was pro-secular had been purged of generals critical of NATO and those who wanted Turkey to look towards the east. I recently encountered families of some detained generals, and the situation is serious.

NOAM CHOMSKY

Yes, I recently made a statement by videoconference to a Freedom of Speech Conference in Istanbul. What's happening is serious and it is particularly saddening because things in the 1990s were horrible. The first time I was there was is in 2000, right at the end of the most awful period. But since then, things were improving. It wasn't great but then it clearly had been improving in a lot of respects. However, since 2005 there has been a series of regressions.

Actually the first time I went to Turkey was to take part in the trial of a publisher who had a Turkish edition of a book of mine. The book had three to four pages on Turkey and therefore was banned. I was critical of the crimes in the 1990s. I went to the trial and accepted his lawyer's request that I be a co-defendant. These are military trials, total farces really. There was a lot of publicity, so the government called off the trial. The publisher was unfortunately picked up later.

The first couple of times I was there it was pretty bad, but it did improve. And the repression now is really serious. But Turkish intellectuals keep struggling; they are unique in the world, I should say. They were consistently opposed to the crimes; they were constantly involved in civil disobedience.

ANDRE VLTCHEK

They are also extremely well informed. I don't know how many of your books they translated—probably dozens.

NOAM CHOMSKY

Many. And the publishers' association is very strong. I went to one of their meetings, and I got some kind of free speech award. The publishers are taking a strong stand against censorship, against repression and are supporting banned and imprisoned writers.

ANDRE VLTCHEK

They are now trying to link with South America. That's almost a must for anybody who writes, to go to South America, to study the situation. So I think the system is shaking. But I am talking about Istanbul and its educated circles, of course; the country, the countryside, is very complex.

NOAM CHOMSKY

It is complex. Diyarbakir, the unofficial capital of the Kurdish regions, is of course a different world, but then Turkey is a unique country.

ANDRE VLTCHEK

Is Israel going to come to its senses and deal with its own demons and give the territory to the Palestinians eventually?

NOAM CHOMSKY

No. Israel won't do anything as long as the U.S. backs it. And why should it? It is getting exactly what it wants. Now it is taking

18 Israeli commandoes training in an abandoned Syrian building
on the occupied Golan Heights. (Copyright Andre Vltchek)

over valuable parts of the West Bank and leaving the remainder
kind of cantonized. Gaza is under tight siege. Every day there
is some new crime.

I just got a report from friends who were with a good NGO
that supports development projects in the West Bank. They
were working in a Palestinian village near Hebron which still
remains a Palestinian town, although there is a group of very
violent, disgraceful settlers there. I have seen these settlers; they
are just shocking. The Israeli army protects them, so they can
beat people up and deface Palestinian homes and overturn fruit
stands, whatever they want. Right near Hebron there is a village
that this NGO was working with, helping the people to plant
a thousand olive trees, a fruit plantation, and the Israeli army
entered one day with no announcement and just uprooted the
olive trees. The army came with an agronomist to ensure it was
done properly, because they wanted to save the trees and move

them over to the Jewish settlement, where they were establishing a park there. Meanwhile they destroyed the entire economic basis of the village and they destroyed homes and so on. And something like that happens every day. Every time you read the Palestinian and Israeli press, there is another story like this. Why should they stop? As long as the U.S. is willing to protect them, they will go on.

ANDRE VLTCHEK

While Israel is oppressing Palestinians, while it occupies their land; while it plays the role of Western outpost in the Middle East, it often appears that the great majority of Israelis are not too interested in politics anymore. Cities like Tel Aviv and Haifa are just extremely rich urban areas with a very high quality of life and almost nothing to suggest that they sit in the conflict zone. A few miles from there the boundaries begin—monstrous walls and barbed-wire fences. But if one sits in posh cafés or concert halls, all that injustice is invisible. And it seems that there is not much internal opposition any more in Israel.

NOAM CHOMSKY

Not much, I think. In the last polls I saw that about two-thirds of the population supports extending the settlements. If you ask about maintaining the settlements it's much higher. And they are all illegal; they concede that they are all illegal. But if you can get away with it, then why stop?

8

Hope in the Most Devastated Places on Earth

ANDRE VLTCHEK

Most of South America is now free, and even some nations in Central America are finally gaining their independence, despite the Monroe Doctrine that still appears to be one of the unchallengeable "gospels" of the American Empire.

But much of the year I am based in Africa and Asia Pacific, and I actually feel that in these parts of the world there is a consolidation of imperial or neo-colonial power: that almost nothing can move freely there anymore. I observe a frightening status quo in most of the countries of Southeast Asia, Sub-Continent and almost all of Africa.

When you look at client states of the West in Southeast Asia—the Philippines, Indonesia, Thailand, and Cambodia— you can see that there is absolutely no discussion about alternative political or social systems. And to some extent, market fundamentalism is deeply rooted even in Singapore, while the social deal between the government, businesses and the people has been gradually dismantled. Brutal feudal clans are de facto rulers of the Philippines: they are buying votes, they are intimidating the opposition, they murder and rape if someone stands in their way. Indonesia is another case of a ruthless feudal society. Thailand is run by a ruinous, corrupt, and medieval monarchy backed by military cronies, which was actually installed after World War II by the West, because the U.S.-born and Swiss-educated monarch was a good candidate for building military bases on the territory of his country, for expansionism and the Vietnam War of the U.S. and its allies. He was also showing some "promising signs" that he would be willing to murder Thai leftists, which he actually did.

And Africa is the most miserable, most destroyed continent in the world. There seems to be no hope here except in South Africa perhaps.

NOAM CHOMSKY

Well, I don't know. If you had been in South America 20 years ago, you would say the same thing. If you had been in the Middle East five years ago, you would say the same thing. Things change. And the capacity of Western force to constrain it had sharply reduced.

ANDRE VLTCHEK

I think one difference between South America and Africa or Southeast Asia is that even some 20 years ago, during the "dark era" in Latin America, there was still that prevailing and powerful desire for an alternative society. I don't see that in Southeast Asia, or in Africa, even in the Middle East. In many of the countries there, from Uganda and Kenya to Indonesia and Philippines, even the so-called "opposition" is often sponsored by the West. It is often that the desire for change involves removal from power of one single person, as was the case with Suharto in Indonesia or Mubarak in Egypt. The social, economic, even political system does not necessarily change. I see great struggle ahead, years, maybe decades of struggle for those parts of the world, to make gains similar to those made by the Latin Americans.

NOAM CHOMSKY

I am less sure about that. I think Latin America looked very much under control—it had been crushed, the liberation theology movement had been smashed and destroyed, the people murdered. There was a fringe of critical commentary but that was really on the fringe, and you can find that in Africa, too. Can they do anything? Well, I don't think we ever know. Nothing looked worse than North Africa but in one or two years it changed.

ANDRE VLTCHEK

One can hope that things are going to change in Africa as they changed in Brazil, in Bolivia, and elsewhere in Latin America. But currently Africa is probably the most devastated place on earth. There seems to be a consolidation of colonial power there, and the horrors that are taking place are often performed by proxies—by local mercenary armies: Rwanda and Uganda plundering DR Congo, Ethiopia and Kenya destroying Somalia. Kenya invaded Somalia in 2011. It appears that Africa is at the lowest point since the official end of colonialism there.

NOAM CHOMSKY

It is the most devastated because it is rich in resources. Right after World War II, the United States was in a position of overwhelming power. Of course the planners understood it, so they laid out elaborate plans for how to organize the world system. The State Department planning staff was headed by George Kennan, who assigned each region of the world what they called "its function." So for example the function of Southeast Asia was to provide the raw materials and resources to the former colonial powers so that they could reconstruct. And then they would be in a position to buy access to U.S. manufacturers, and so on.

When they got to Africa, Kennan wrote that the U.S. was not interested in Africa, so it could be handed over to the Europeans to "exploit"—his word—for their reconstruction. So it was handed to Europe to exploit, so that they could reconstruct and become an active part of the U.S.-dominated system and a market for U.S. goods and investments and so on. Africa has to be exploited. Well in more recent time the U.S. has had second thoughts about that and says it must exploit Africa too. So the U.S. has begun to move into Africa, because it gets a lot of oil from there and also uranium and other minerals.

So it's left not just to the Europeans to exploit; now the U.S. is going to make sure that it does too. But the idea of Africa as just a source of exploitation was second nature. Kennan is regarded as a great humanist but no one would ever mention something like this, because it's normal; why should we mention it?

ANDRE VLTCHEK

Of course now France is taking those words for what they were supposed to mean. It is incredible the role France is beginning to play across Africa, from Djibouti to Somalia, from Western Sahara to Libya.*

NOAM CHOMSKY

The French role has indeed generally been terrible. The French supported Ben Ali, the Tunisian dictator, long after the uprisings began. They were kind of embarrassed by it finally, but they are a horrible ruler in Africa and it is still persisting.

ANDRE VLTCHEK

The French still have their foreign legions all over the place; I recently saw French legionnaires in Djibouti. And they have been historically extremely brutal. There were French mercenaries in Djibouti being trained for operations all over the continent. And now with Libya I think we are waking up to a nightmare; realizing what a powerful role France is ready to play again ... powerful and tremendously destructive for African people. I am sure you can offer many other examples.

NOAM CHOMSKY

The Western Sahara case is interesting. I mean the people there, the Sahrawi, are real unpeople! It was the last official colony in Africa, so it is under UN administration, for decolonization ... But as soon as decolonization was declared in 1975, it was invaded by Morocco, which is a French client. Morocco went in, threw out the independent government and began settling the country with Moroccans, so that if there is ever

---

* Since our conversation we have seen the dreadful invasion of Mali by French troops, and foreign legionnaires, recruited, paid, and trained by France.

a referendum, as the UN has demanded, the Moroccans would be able to dominate the referendum. There has been extensive resistance by guerrilla forces and they keep bringing claims and charges to the United Nations.

The most recent one was right at the outset of the Arab Spring. In fact the Arab Spring began in the Western Sahara, before Tunisia. Tent cities were constructed as acts of non-violent resistance in Western Sahara. Moroccan forces of course quickly moved in and demolished them. The Sahrawi brought it to the United Nations, which is responsible. France blocked any investigation, backed by the U.S., because their client was doing it. This was not seen as part of the repression in the Arab Spring, but it's actually the first step.

ANDRE VLTCHEK

There is, as we mentioned, the war in Congo, where the country is being plundered by both Rwanda and Uganda on behalf of Western interests—the worst genocide since World War II, an absolute cover-up, gaining hardly any media coverage in the West!

And I've just finished filming another awful subject: the Dadaab Refugee Camp, holding mainly Somali refugees in northern Kenya. It is the biggest refugee camp in the world with approximately 600,000 people living in the desert. Somalia has been totally destabilized, destroyed, broken to pieces; its coast allegedly poisoned by the EU waste ... My friend, a former Kenyan member of parliament, told me that while Kenya helped to sponsor Somali peace agreements in the past, the West always torpedoed all such initiatives, because it never wanted to accept any Islamic nationalist ruler there.

NOAM CHOMSKY

Yes, and they supported the Ethiopian invasion, that has overthrown the Islamic Courts during the one brief period of relative peace. One of the so-called great achievements was when the U.S. destroyed al-Barakaat, a major charity that was "supporting terrorism." They later conceded that this was an error. Actually the charity happened to have been the main charity that was funding a lot of Somali life; Somali banks, Somali businesses, sustenance to the population. When it was criminalized, all that stopped, so that was another blow to the very fragile survival of the country that is being beaten on all sides. Actually Europe is helping too, by dumping toxic waste into the ocean off the coasts of Somalia, killing off the fishing grounds and then complaining that the people turned to piracy.

19   Girls in a primary school at Dadaab Refugee Camp, Kenya.
(Copyright Yayoi Segi)

ANDRE VLTCHEK

Yes, all that is taking place in and around Somalia is awful. And the West has its own Rottweiler there—Djibouti—that has turned into some sort of U.S. and French military base, converting its desert to the training grounds for the French legions. I never saw such an appalling, over-militarized place anywhere on earth as Djibouti! It is polluted, aggressive, and subservient. There, you check into their Sheraton Hotel, and in the morning you find out that the German army has its own cook there, making the breakfast!

And there is of course West Africa, which has become a French playground. Last time I went to Dakar, Senegal, I witnessed French military maneuvers: a helicopter carrier, destroyers and other military vessels were passing right by the historic Gorée island, which used to serve as transit point for African slaves exported all over the world by French colonial rulers. Very symbolic, I would say—and no shame. If there are any positive developments in sub-Saharan Africa, it is in South Africa.

NOAM CHOMSKY

You know better than I do that South Africa changed for the better after the end of apartheid, but not on class issues. That remained pretty well fixed. You may have black faces in the limousines, but for the poor majority, miserable conditions remain.

ANDRE VLTCHEK

But it was not only because of the ANC. It was, at least partially, because of the conditions on how to run the economy that were enforced on the first ANC government from abroad. These were actually people who spent too much time in jail and didn't know much about the outside world. Naomi Klein has argued that they were tricked in similar ways to Gorbachev. (There were treats of punitive actions in case the ANC would not adopt the financial and economic measures professed by the West.)

NOAM CHOMSKY

I am skeptical about that. I think they felt that they had a right to the prerogatives enjoyed by the elites. And they very quickly recreated a neo-liberal society. I don't think they were forced to do that. My feeling is that the same thing happened elsewhere. Take as an example Sandinista Nicaragua. The leadership was from the Nicaraguan elite. As soon as they got power they wanted to live the way elites lived... later there was the Piñata, as you know ... and they did. Then you get this tremendous corruption, where Humberto Ortega owned a huge walled estate in the middle of Managua, and so on. Revolutionary leaders are typically from amongst the elite. They fight courageously, and it is not easy to overthrow a dictatorship; a lot of people get killed; in South Africa people were tortured and exiled. But when the leaders come into power they easily move into the same patterns as those people they have replaced.

I was in Cape Town shortly after the fall of apartheid, and was able to meet with dissidents. I remember one black activist came in and described how he had just came from a cocktail party at a fancy new hotel downtown. All the rich people were there, and they were now part of it and everybody was quite cheerful about that. That seemed to be the mood generally, but less so amongst people of South Asian background—they seemed to be much more militant. They were still talking about Steve Biko and the promise of the movement that had not been achieved. I don't want to say too much based on limited personal experiences, but from that and from what I read it seems to me that the anti-apartheid movement quite easily moved into the neo-liberal framework of empowerment of elites that marginalizes the majority of the population.

ANDRE VLTCHEK

They didn't have it that easy though. I was in Cape Town during the Commission of Truth and Reconciliation, and there was an enormous outflow of white professionals, who were the only ones allowed to run the country during apartheid. All those white professionals moved to Canada, Australia, the United States; and the economy suffered, GDP went down, the country was being drained. And the more reforms the ANC suggested, the more professionals, especially whites, would threaten to leave the country.

NOAM CHOMSKY

But that's routine. When Chavez came in, for example, there was huge capital flight out of Venezuela. When he was briefly overthrown, it started coming back in. The same happened in Haiti with Aristide. As long as capital flow is free, that's going to be a major weapon against any reform. It is even discussed in the technical economics literature. They talk about how governments have "dual constituencies." They have their own population but they also have the domestic and international investor community which carries out a "moment by moment referendum" on government policies and if it doesn't like the policies, it bars them by speculating against the currency, by capital flight and by other measures. And the second constituency, the international investment community, typically wins out over the population. Not always, but they are a very powerful force. However, this power can be limited too. Take Korea, during its period of great economic growth: they not only barred capital flight, but you could get the death penalty for it. There are things that can be done.

We must remember that there have been significant achievements for liberation movements, even in the most devastated of places. Take the Indonesian invasion and occupation of East Timor in 1975. That was one of the worst atrocities in the post-war period; it is as close to a genocide as anything that happened. The U.S. supported it: Britain and Australia supported it. Other Western powers too. People campaigned against the occupation from within those supporting Western countries—I was very much involved in organizing this, as were you and many others, but we could not break through. Finally, in 1999, after the huge Dili massacre which drove 250,000 people out of the city, there was enough domestic and international pressure so that Clinton ordered the Indonesian generals to stop—and they turned on a dime. Within a day it was over. What that tells you is that it could have been stopped 25 years earlier, but there wasn't the pressure. It was interesting how this was portrayed in the West. After the Indonesian military left, a UN peacekeeping force came in, Australian-led, and that is now described as one of the great humanitarian interventions.

ANDRE VLTCHEK

There is also a second interpretation, which is that Australia discovered gas at the bottom of the sea, and that it would be easier for them to deal with weak East Timor than with huge Indonesia.

NOAM CHOMSKY

The Australians knew about the gas all along. And in fact Australia and Indonesia had made a pact to allow Australia access to what they called the oil of "the Indonesian province of East Timor." That was the only official recognition of East Timor as an Indonesian province. There is a photo—which is famous in Australia—of Gareth Evans, the Australian foreign minister at the time, signing the pact with Ali Alatas, his Indonesian counterpart. They were drinking and there were high-fives and all was very exultant, because Australia had obtained the right to the oil of the Indonesian province of East Timor. In the light of Australia's shameful role in supporting the Indonesian invasion and atrocities, during his tenure in particular, Evans was pressed on this by the activist movement in Australia, and his response was "the world is an unfair place, littered with cases of acquisition by force," and this is just another one so it doesn't matter. And if it was near genocide, well, things happen.

Now Gareth Evans is the hero of the "responsibility to protect" movement. *The Economist* ran an article with a picture of him sitting in grief, because so many terrible things are happening in the world despite the "bold but passionate" dedication to protect the vulnerable that has been his guide throughout his life. But they didn't publish the picture of him with Ali Alatas, savoring his support for virtual genocide in East Timor because, after all, the world is littered by such cases. Well, Australia had access to the gas.

Australia is a very interesting case. If you look back at World War II, the Japanese were moving south, and they were probably planning to invade Australia. Timor was in the way. There were a couple of hundred Australian commandoes on the island who were fighting off the Japanese invasion, and the Timorese strongly supported the Australians and I think about 60,000 Timorese were killed. People in Australia remembered that. You know: "my grandfather was there," "my uncle was there." There was an undercurrent of anger about the way Australia treated East Timor. It became quite an active movement. I was there in the mid-1990s, at the invitation of Jose Ramos Horta [foreign minister in the "Democratic Republic of East Timor" government in exile], to speak to the East Timor Refugees Association. They had their first main meetings then, and there was lots of public support with big city meetings in Sydney and Melbourne and so on. But Evans and the government nevertheless went ahead with the deal.

But in September 1999, it broke when Clinton switched his position. There was a lot of a pressure on Clinton; incidentally, some of it was coming from influential figures on the U.S. right who were close to the Catholic community. East Timor is a Catholic country. That was one factor, but there was also international protest. It tells you a lot—they couldn't maintain support for the occupation of East Timor. That's one case but there are many others, I think.

ANDRE VLTCHEK

The Kennedys were also involved in East Timor towards the end. When I was arrested in East Timor after the Ermera Massacre in 1996, and sent to the intelligence office and tortured there, I was released only after the intervention of the U.S. Embassy. Then I went to Jakarta and I was met by some Embassy person who said: "Well, this is a good time to highlight the issue of East Timor, because the Kennedy family is getting very interested and involved, and they are becoming very critical of the Indonesian occupation of East Timor."

After the Indonesian troops left, I can testify that the leadership of Timor Leste was going through an absolutely terrible time regarding their dealing with Australia and the so-called international community, in relation to the gas deposits and the way Australia was allowed to openly bully them.

NOAM CHOMSKY

I think one of the things that has really changed U.S. relations with Indonesia is when Suharto could not hold on any longer in 1998. There was a huge public uprising, student protests of all kinds, and the IMF was unhappy with Suharto. A picture was circulated all over Indonesia of the French head of the IMF standing there with his hands crossed and a humbled Suharto sitting as the IMF ordered Suharto to carry out certain policies, and Suharto bowed. Right at that point Madeleine Albright, Secretary of State, wrote a letter to Suharto saying that "it's time for the democratic transition in Indonesia." And about four hours later Suharto resigned.

ANDRE VLTCHEK

Yes, but I have my own theory. I was living with the students at Trisakti University during the uprisings. I was not impressed at all, because Trisakti is an upper-class university, and the students were not really pushing for revolution, for fundamental change in Indonesian society. They just wanted Suharto to step down, as if the resignation of one single man could overhaul and improve the entire system. Also, whatever happened during that period of very profound economic and financial crisis, Suharto was until the end insisting on holding some key Indonesian industries in his own and his family's hands—not in state hands, of course, but neither was he ready to privatize them or sell them to foreigner investors.

I think it was too much for the IMF and for the West. They actually wanted an even more right-wing government to take over Indonesia, and to have almost all industries and natural resources go to foreign companies, mostly those in the West. That eventually happened, because after Suharto stepped down, the corruption exploded from just the upper ranks to all ranks of society, and almost everything got to be privatized. Suddenly the whole country with its enormous natural resources was for grabs. It was just a matter of price.

It is very significant that in Egypt, for instance, Western advisers are propagating the Indonesian model. Mass media are also suggesting that Arab Spring countries should closely follow the Indonesian economic and "democratic" model. It is of course never mentioned and never explained that Indonesia has been a collapsing country, that there is not one political party who would be ready to defend the interests of the majority living in misery, and that the lauded economic growth is achieved by the plunder of natural resources by a small group of elite.

9

The Decline of
U.S. Power

ANDRE VLTCHEK

I see U.S. and Europe as the Empire that is consolidating its power all over the world. Some pockets of resistance are still there: like Latin America, China, even Iran. But the space for maneuvering for the rest of the world is diminishing; at least from my experience, gained on the ground. I know that you are much more optimistic on this....

NOAM CHOMSKY

The peak of U.S. power was in the 1940s. It's been declining ever since. In 1945 the U.S. had half the world's wealth, a position of overwhelming security, control of the hemisphere, both the Atlantic and Pacific oceans, most of the other sides of the oceans. Other industrial societies were devastated and destroyed. The U.S. was occupying Japan and there was essential control in Western Europe. The first task of the U.S. and Britain when they moved onto the European continent was to destroy the anti-fascist resistance and weaken the powerful labor movements and to reinstitute pretty much the traditional regimes with fascist collaborators, and so on.

That started in 1943, when they moved into Italy and then continued elsewhere, with particular brutality in Greece, regarded as part of the periphery of the energy-rich Middle East. Germany was a great concern because they knew Germany would be the center of the industrial system in Europe. So it was a real problem, what to do with Germany. The British and Americans were concerned with what they regarded as the contagion coming from East Germany. George Kennan, one of the chief planners, had a nice phrase: he argued that we need to "wall off" West Germany from the Eastern Zone, to prevent the spread of radical thought about labor movement organizing, and so on. And Germany was pretty much reconstituted on traditional terms. Labor unions were very much undermined.

In France strike breakers were needed to smash the unions. Partly this was just the normal process of breaking up organized labor. But dockworkers in Marseilles were interfering with the shipments of supplies and arms to the French in Indochina, to help in the French attempt to re-conquer Indochina. Well if you are going to break up strikes and smash up the labor movement, you need somebody to do it. This is something the mafia are good at. But the Nazis ran a tight ship and had pretty much destroyed the mafia: they didn't like the competition. And so the U.S. reconstituted it in Sicily and in southern France (the Corsican Mafia). Well, the mafia won't break up unions for nothing—you have to offer them a payoff. The payoff was to give them control over the heroin industry. That's the famous French Connection, which developed in southern France and goes on throughout the world.

Wherever there is subversion, intervention and so on you get the drug system following it for pretty good reasons. And if say the CIA is overthrowing the government, subverting the unions and so on, first of all they need personnel and then they need black money, untraceable money. When put together properly it works well and it's common throughout the world. The historian Alfred McCoy has written the essential work on this [*The Politics of Heroin*].

The same happened to Japan. Douglas MacArthur (the de facto leader of Japan, 1945–48) allowed democratic development in Japan during the early post-war years. He allowed union organizing, democratic initiatives and so on. When the liberals in Washington learned about this, they were horrified and they moved in 1947. That was what was called "the reverse course" and they smashed all this up and restored the power of the big enterprises. Essentially they restored something like the fascist system.

ANDRE VLTCHEK

They used people like Shoriki Matsutaro, who was a CIA agent and the president of the Yomiuri group, an enormous media company in Japan.

NOAM CHOMSKY

And they installed old Japanese war criminals. That's what happened all over the world. Anyway, that was the peak of U.S. power and then it started to decline. The independence of China in 1949 was a major blow, as China was considered a crucial part of the world order that the U.S. was trying to reconstitute. There has been a lot of talk in the U.S. over who was responsible for the loss of China—it goes on right to the present. This is an interesting way of looking at it—we lost China because we owned it and somebody caused it to be lost, you know. Well that was the first case of decline, and that immediately set off serious concerns about the potential loss of Southeast Asia, and that's when U.S. policy shifted towards Southeast Asia.

In the early years after the war, there was a conflict of policy initiatives. The U.S. was opposed to the old imperial systems in the region because they blocked U.S. economic and other interventions, but they were also opposed to nationalist movements developing. So conflicting policies were taking shape in different places. In Indonesia, for example, after the 1948 Madiun massacre, the U.S. decided to support Sukarno [the first president of Indonesia, 1945–67]. But in Indochina, by the late 1940s the U.S. was vacillating, and it shifted towards supporting the French re-conquest. But what they were really concerned about was not Indochina, if you read the documents, but Indonesia. Indonesia had rich resources, it was a big important country, while Indochina did not amount to much. But they were afraid that, as planners put it, "the rot would spread" from Vietnam to Thailand and even to Indonesia, and possibly even to Japan. The U.S. was concerned that Japan might "accommodate" to an independent Southeast Asia, becoming its commercial and industrial center. That would in effect mean that the U.S. had lost its Pacific phase of World War II, which was fought to prevent Japan from developing what they called a New Order in Asia. Roughly like that. The U.S. in 1950 was not prepared to lose World War II, so that's when they began a massive support of the French in Indochina.

And then in 1958 Eisenhower carried out the biggest intervention so far in the post-war period: to try to split off the outer islands of Indonesia, where most of the natural resources are, to get them under U.S. control. The U.S. were also concerned over too much democracy in Indonesia. If you read U.S. records from that period, you can see that they were concerned that Sukarno's government was allowing political participation by the PKI (Communist Party of Indonesia), which scholarship understands to have been basically the party of the poor. They were afraid that if this continued, if there was a democratic process, the PKI would gain control. But the U.S. intervention failed. And we know what happened in 1965.

ANDRE VLTCHEK

The U.S.-sponsored coup, massacres of Communists, intellectuals and the Chinese minority. About three million people died.

NOAM CHOMSKY

I haven't heard figures that high, but whatever it was, it was awful.

ANDRE VLTCHEK

The current president, Susilo Bambang Yudhoyono, was married to a daughter of Sarwo Edhie Wibowo, a notorious special forces "Red Beret" general, who loved to brag that he and his mates had killed three million people after 1965. He was one of the few who confirmed three million.

In my opinion it was an extremely important event for the West, because Western governments and companies were testing the ground for what could be applied years later in

20   Anti-Communist propaganda in Indonesia.
(Copyright Andre Vltchek)

many other parts of the world. In a way it was not only a coup,
but also an economic experiment. It was an opportunity to
implement an extreme pro-market economic system force-fed by
the University of California at Berkeley through its Indonesian
collaborators at the client-institution of the University of
Indonesia. Even before the coup, Berkeley had set up an
alternative team of Indonesian economists at the University
of Indonesia. Sometime later the Chicago School of Economics
was trying to forge the same unholy alliance with the University
of Chile—but the University of Chile refused and then the
Universidad Católica in Santiago was contacted and accepted.
So in Chile before the 1973 coup, just as in Indonesia before
the 1965 coup, there was already a fundamentalist pro-market
alternative economic system in place.

NOAM CHOMSKY

You are right to stress that developments in South America and in Southeast Asia were happening in parallel. That's usually overlooked. It should be a priority in analysis of policy planning. Uncontroversially, Washington planners have global concerns. These crucial perspectives tend to be ignored, I think, on the useful assumption that the U.S. is not really an actor in world affairs. Washington reacts to others, devoted to "doing good" in its naive and clumsy ways.

A year before Suharto's coup came the Brazilian coup, and Brazil was the most important country in South America. The Brazilian coup was planned by Kennedy's administration and took place a few months after the assassination. It is an interesting illustration of the decline of U.S. power, I think. The policies of the government that the U.S. helped to overthrow, the João Belchior Marques Goulart government, were not very different from Lula's policies, but now Lula [Luiz Inácio Lula da Silva, president of Brazil, 2003–11] is the darling of the West. At that time they were so intolerable that the government had to be overthrown and a really vicious military dictatorship established. That was the first one. That did set off a domino effect—Brazil is important—as government after government collapsed. And then Chicago-trained economists came in.

ANDRE VLTCHEK

In a way I think the aftershocks of the Indonesian coup was later felt even in some faraway places like South Africa and Russia under Yeltsin. The experiment worked, and the West replicated it from Moscow to Pretoria to Kigali in Rwanda.

NOAM CHOMSKY

And in Chile too. It was quite overt—the right wing were declaring their Jakarta solution.

ANDRE VLTCHEK

I have talked to many people from Allende's government, now very old people, and they said that they were shouted at before the coup: "Comrades, be careful, Jakarta is coming!" And they told me: "We didn't know what exactly they meant by 'Jakarta'. We knew it is the capital of Indonesia but we didn't realize the bloodbath that they were actually promising."

A few years ago I made a feature documentary film, *Terlena—Breaking of the Nation*, about the 1965 coup in Indonesia and its aftermath. When I showed the film in Montevideo, Uruguay, and especially later in Santiago de Chile, survivors of the 1973 coup would come to the stage, crying, hugging me, saying: "We didn't know . . . it was the same here in Chile as it was in Indonesia . . . the same!"

NOAM CHOMSKY

It was interesting to see the U.S., British, and Australian reactions. The massacre in Indonesia was described pretty accurately, so the *New York Times* for example wrote about what they called a "staggering mass slaughter." Their leading liberal correspondent, James Reston, had a column praising the events as "A gleam of light in Asia"—that was the way a leading journal in the West described it. And he and the editors praised the U.S. government for keeping the U.S. role under wraps, so that the "moderate" Indonesian generals, as they called them, could take credit for having done this by themselves; they didn't want to discredit them by saying "look we helped you out." It was the same in Australia and Britain; there was unconstrained euphoria.

A comparison that can't help coming to mind, with rather different implications, is Cuba's handling of its decisive role in the liberation of Africa. The Cubans kept silent about it, wanting domestic African leaders to have the credit and prestige. It was all brought to light recently by the outstanding diplomatic historian Piero Gleijeses, at Johns Hopkins. It would be nice to see the comparison developed somewhere.

McGeorge Bundy, who was the national security advisor for Kennedy and Johnson, reflected years later that it might have been a good idea to have ended the war in Vietnam in 1965. Through the coup in Indonesia the U.S. had effectively won its Southeast Asian war. By 1965 Vietnam was a wreck, it wasn't going to be a model for anyone, and they had succeeded in gaining control of Indonesia, which was their main concern. And then dictatorships were established in all surrounding regions preventing the spread of "the rot"—the rot of successful independent development, which might be a model for others, a leading theme of Cold War history. Henry Kissinger's imagery was that these nationalist movements are a virus, which can spread contagion—he applied this to Allende as well. His government was a virus that can spread contagion all the way to southern Europe; if people can see that there is a parliamentary road to social reform, that is very dangerous. Brezhnev apparently agreed with him, fearing the spread of "EuroCommunism," a form of social democracy and a competitor to Soviet tyranny under the name of "Communism."

If you have a virus that's going to spread contagion, you have to destroy the virus and inoculate those who might be infected, and that was done in Southeast Asia and in Latin America at the same time. It was in the 1960s that the main wave of repression started building across Latin America; the Brazilian dictatorship was established which ran through to the 1980s; then other dominoes fell, leading finally to Reagan's murderous wars in Central America. And in Southeast Asia there was Ferdinand Marcos in the Philippines; Thailand had a dictatorship; Suharto was in Indonesia and Burmese democracy was pretty much smashed, with effects going on still today. And it all suddenly looked pretty good when you stopped the contagion and you destroyed the virus.

Nevertheless, U.S. power was declining and by 1970 American share of world wealth was down to about 25 percent, which is enormous but not 50 percent, as it was in 1945. And the world was considered economically tri-polar. The major economic centers were in Europe (centred in West Germany), in North America (principally the U.S.), and East Asia (centred around Japan)—the last of the three was already the most dynamic economic area in the world. And since then the U.S. has declined further. In the last ten years, the loss of South America is very significant, for that was considered completely safe. So safe they didn't talk about it. And now the U.S. has virtually no influence in South America apart from Colombia—there is only a tiny bit around Peru. The U.S. is trying to restore it, but nothing like it used to be. We talked about the Cartagena conference (the Summit of the Americas)—that was a very dramatic illustration of the loss of American power in the hemisphere. The U.S. was isolated on every major issue, and probably won't even be part of the hemispheric meetings next time.

The Arab Spring is another concern. If the Arab Spring actually moves towards developing some kind of functioning democracies in the region, the U.S. and its allies would be in real trouble. It is clear that public opinion in the Arab world is very opposed to the U.S. and its allies, so there have been very major efforts to keep democracy in the region under control.

U.S. power is still overwhelming and scarcely challenged, but it is declining. They cannot now do things like what they used to do. They can't just overthrow governments in Latin America. They don't have the military force to intervene elsewhere, in the Middle East and so on.

ANDRE VLTCHEK

But they did. The Obama administration managed to overthrow two left-wing governments in Latin America recently: in Honduras and in Paraguay. I agree with you that, proportionally, the U.S. controls a smaller chunk of the global economy than it did after World War II, but now the Empire combines both the U.S. and EU, and even, arguably, Japan. If these three powers are combined, the situation is not too different from the end of World War II.

NOAM CHOMSKY

I see your point, but I think it may underestimate European and Japanese independence. And there's more. If you go back to the early 1950s, U.S. planners were quite concerned that Europe might become what was called a third force. It might move towards some kind of independence from the two major superpowers. That was one of the great concerns, and one of the methods for preventing that was NATO.

NATO was presented as a military force to defend Europe from the Russian hordes. It was never very easy to fully accept that, but it was very dramatic to see what happened in 1989 with the fall of the Berlin Wall. What is NATO for if there are no more Russian hordes? The doctrines should have led to the prediction that NATO would be dismantled, but what happened is that NATO expanded.

George Bush senior and James Baker made a compact with Mikhail Gorbachev that they would permit a unified Germany to join a Western military alliance, which is no joke from Russia's point of view. But in return, they said NATO would not move "one inch to the East." Well, immediately they moved to the East and Gorbachev was pretty upset. He was told that this was just a verbal agreement. If you are naive enough to take us at our word, it's your problem. There was nothing on paper. So they moved to the East and continued. Now NATO is a U.S.-run global intervention force. It has an official mandate for controlling the international energy system, sea lanes, pipelines, and so on.

The military budget of 1989 was very interesting. The Bush administration also had a new defense strategy: "National Security Strategy," saying that the U.S. has to keep a huge military system, not because of the Russians, because they aren't around anymore, but because of what was called the

21   Futenma U.S. Marine Corps base in Okinawa, Japan.
(Copyright Andre Vltchek)

"technological sophistication" of Third World powers. Secondly it said the U.S. had to maintain the "defense industrial base." That's a euphemism, referring to high-tech industry, developed substantially out of government initiative and expenditures, usually through the Pentagon.

But the most interesting part was about the Middle East. They said that the U.S. has to maintain intervention forces directed at the Middle East, where the serious problems faced could not have been "laid at the Kremlin's door." In other words, contrary to 50 years of lying, it wasn't because the U.S. was afraid of the Russians, but because of the threat of "radical nationalism"— independent nationalism. And now they came clean, clouds had lifted. But it made no difference, because nobody reported it and even scholarship didn't study it: I think I may have been one of the few people who even reported it. That crucial moment, with the collapse of the global enemy, is exactly where you would look if you want to understand the Cold War. You would look at what happened when it was over.

So Europe largely follows the U.S. lead and rarely takes independent initiatives. It's particularly true of Britain. If you read British Foreign Office records from the 1940s, it's clear they recognized that their day in the sun was over and that Britain would have to be the "junior partner" of the United States, and sometimes treated in a very humiliating way. A striking example was in 1962, the time of the Cuban missile crisis. The Kennedy planners were making very dangerous choices and pursuing policies which they thought had a good chance of leading to nuclear war, and they knew that Britain would be wiped out. The U.S. wouldn't, because Russia's missiles couldn't reach there, but Britain would be wiped out.

The planners weren't telling Britain what they were doing. Harold Macmillan, the British prime minister, was desperately trying to find out what was going on in Washington and all that he could learn was what British intelligence was able to pick up. And right at that time a senior American advisor said in an internal discussion that the British shouldn't be told, that the U.S. can't trust the British. One described the true nature of the famous "special relationship": "the British are our lieutenant. The fashionable term is partner." And that's what the British are. Continental Europeans are even less—they follow along, but they are a little worrisome because they can't be entirely relied upon. In fact, none of them can be firmly relied on. They have the capacity to pursue an independent course, and sometimes have.

ANDRE VLTCHEK

And yet, United States foreign policy now is fully based on the colonial culture of Europe.

NOAM CHOMSKY

But it is also the U.S. culture. One of the main historians of imperialism, Bernard Porter, pointed out a couple years ago that we should be careful about what he called "the salt-water fallacy"—that imperialism means crossing salt-water. He means that it is no different if you cross the Irish Sea or if you cross the Mississippi, it is imperialism either way. So the conquest of the national territory in the United States is not called imperialism. But that's a linguistic decision. Of course it was the conquest of somebody else's territory and land, first of all the native population, but then half of Mexico (all the Southwest and West was Mexican territory, that's why you have city names like San Francisco and San Diego), and it's only after this phase of American imperialism came to its end that you start getting overseas imperialism. Cuba in 1898, also Puerto Rico, Hawaii, the Philippines, and so on.

It is a special form of imperialism that developed in the so-called "Anglosphere"—English-speaking countries that began as British colonies. It is different from conventional imperialism, because they didn't just rule the countries that they conquered or administered, they displaced the native population or exterminated them and then settled there. There was the same process in Australia and Canada, and almost the same in New Zealand except the Maori resisted so are still somehow integrated in the society, but its the same structure. In Tasmania the indigenous population was decimated even more than happened in the U.S.; some claim completely, although I've heard from descendants who deny it. And this cannot be acknowledged within the doctrinal system.

The United Nations has a Rapporteur on Indigenous Rights, who decided to look at indigenous rights in the United States, and of course they found the kind of horror stories that are typical for the Indian reservations. They came out with the report, and there was almost no comment on it, it couldn't get reported. The only coverage I could find was on Fox News, the right-wing channel, who were furious when it came out. It was interesting to read the very derogatory commentary about those miserable creatures at the United Nations: "What right do they have to poke in our affairs, we'll get rid of the United Nations," and so on. The idea that anyone should look at indigenous rights in the United States is apparently unacceptable. The imperial mentality remains very much in place, but the capacity to implement the policies is sharply reduced. You see it all over the world.

ANDRE VLTCHEK

Do you think there is any way that the American people could come to understand the negative impact their country has had on the rest of the world? That people would begin realizing the damage they had done?

NOAM CHOMSKY

The 1960s had a real civilizing effect on American society. There are things that can be done in the mainstream now that would have been very unlikely in the 1950s or 1960s, which was a highly conformist period. I was in Greensboro, North Carolina recently giving some talks about Israel–Palestine. Five or ten years ago you just couldn't talk about that topic. I would have had police protection even at MIT. Now there are huge crowds, lots of interest, wide concerns about U.S. policy.

There has been a growing willingness to pay attention to the consequences of U.S. actions. I don't want to say it overwhelms the society, but it's increasing and substantial. Take the two core crimes in the history of the United States— the virtual extermination of the indigenous population (to borrow the terms of the Founders) and slavery. Until the 1960s even professional anthropologists were saying that there were very few American Indians, and they were hunter-gatherers, wandering around. It wasn't until about 1975, I guess, that the first serious book came out undermining the mythology, called *The Invasion of America* by Francis Jennings. There had been others but they were suppressed—Helen Hunt Jackson wrote a very revealing book about what has been done to the Native American population in the 1880s—it was still going on right at that time—but I think maybe 200 copies were printed and it quickly disappeared. It was resurrected in the 1970s/80s, but still only a few people have read it. Francis Jennings was not a professional academic anthropologist; he was the director of a Native American Museum. He did a lot of research and brought up all sorts of things, which had a big effect on the movements that grew out of the 1960s; there was a readiness for thinking about this.

Things were very different from when I was growing up in the 1930s and 40s. My family was left-liberal, some with a radical background, but my friends and I would run around the woods playing cowboys and Indians. We were the cowboys, we would kill the Indians, you know. By the 1960s and the 1970s that was less the case. In 1969 I had a daughter who was ten years old, and I was poking through her school books. One of them was called *Exploring New England* and it was leading the children through early New England history. There was an older man who was a guide, and the protagonist was a young boy. And this older man was showing him all those wonderful things that happened in the settlement of New England. I was wondering to myself, "how are you going to treat things like the Pequot Massacre?" which was a horrible massacre where savage colonists killed all the women and children. It was actually depicted pretty accurately, and they had the boy react: "I wish I was a man and had been there." He was saying that he should slaughter women and children, and drive them out and take over their lands. I showed it to my wife. She was scandalized of course and went to talk to the teacher, and the teacher asked her what the problem was. She showed her the passage. The teacher looked at it and didn't see any spelling mistakes! She didn't understand what the problem was at all. And so my wife asked her: "Do you think it's right to be teaching children things like this? In particular right now, you know, with the My Lai massacre on the front pages." The teacher's reaction was: "Well, not everyone is liberal the way you are." So most of us think it's quite fine to exterminate people and take their lands. That was in 1969 and not in the backward areas of the rural South, but in liberal New England. That has now changed—I am sure you couldn't have textbooks like that now—and the picture of Native Americans has changed.

It is similar with regard to the history of slavery, which had also been suppressed. Now the true narratives are beginning to come out. It has been assumed that after the Civil War things got better, that the slaves were freed, and so on. The first work is just beginning to come out, outside of scholarly studies, showing that after slavery was formally eliminated, it was essentially reintroduced. Ten years after the Civil War, after the amendments and so on, there was a compact between the North and the South which essentially enabled the South to reestablish a form of slavery by criminalizing black life. So almost anything that a black male was doing could be regarded as criminal, like standing at the street corner or looking at a white woman, or whatever. Pretty soon they had a large black male population in jail, and they became a very good labor force. That's a lot better than having slaves—if you have a slave you have to take care of him; they are your property. If you get your workforce from the jails, you don't have to take care of them, they are not going to strike, they are not going to ask for better wages. A good part of the American industrial revolution was based on that. It goes almost to World War II and—this is just beginning to be recognized—it has some similarity with what's happening right now with the criminalization of much of the black labor force under the racist "drug war" that assumed its recent form since Reagan.

But consider the Vietnam War. As we discussed earlier, we have recently had the 50th Anniversary of the launching of the war. When the war started, I began to give talks about it—I was giving talks in people's living room with two or three neighbors, or at a church with four people showing up. When we tried to have meetings on the Vietnam War at MIT in the early 1960s, we'd have to bring together half of a dozen topics… Venezuela, Vietnam, Israel… and then maybe ten people would show up.

In Boston, maybe the most liberal city in the country, the first effort to have a public demonstration on the Boston Common, which is the standard place for meeting, was in October 1965, an international day of protest. It was broken up violently, mostly by students. I was supposed to be one of the speakers, but the speakers could not be heard. The only reason we were not physically attacked was because there were a lot of state police around—not because they liked the demonstration, but because they didn't want to have people killed on the Boston Common. The *Boston Globe,* a major liberal newspaper, the most liberal in the country, published a bitter denunciation of the demonstrators the next day alongside a picture of a wounded war veteran. Radio was full of terrible denunciations of the criminal activities of those who were questioning the valor and nobility of our boys saving Vietnam, on and on like that.

Earlier my wife had taken our two little girls to a women's demonstration in Concord, a quiet suburb, with a long pacifist tradition. Nothing much, they were just standing with signs. The women and girls were attacked by an angry crowd, throwing tin cans and tomatoes at them.

And then after five years of war, in March 1966, there was another international day of protest. We realized we could not have a public one so we had it in a church. The church was attacked—again, tin cans and tomatoes were thrown, and again with public applause. Later things changed, but it was slow.

ANDRE VLTCHEK

Barack Obama's background is very much connected to the U.S. intelligence service and especially the ones operating in two places: Kenya and Indonesia, where he spent his childhood. Obama's father was recruited by Tom Mboya, a Kenyan right-wing politician from the Luo tribe, who was very close to the U.S. government. They went to Hawaii where they were trained or educated, and later sent back to Africa. There Mboya and Obama's father helped Kenyatta, the first President of Kenya, to get rid of all the left-wing influences and to sideline the progressive leader Oginga Odinga.

NOAM CHOMSKY

Yes. I am not sure how much contact he had with his father actually.

ANDRE VLTCHEK

Not much—his father died when he was young, but he had a little contact. His father was an alcoholic, he had several car accidents in Kenya, and he was disabled for most of his later years. But it wasn't only Obama's Kenyan father who was on an anti-left crusade.

President Obama spent part of his childhood in Indonesia. His mother remarried after she met an Indonesian army officer who was being trained in Hawaii. He was called home to help with the aftermath of the 1965 coup. Obama's mother and the young Obama actually moved to Indonesia just a short time after the coup; he grew up in Menteng, an elite neighborhood of

Jakarta, and so he is known there even now as Barry of Menteng. It was a solid upper-middle to upper-class neighborhood, and the family lived inside the military compound. Even now he speaks very warmly about his childhood, which in reality coincides with torture, mass murder, rapes and disappearances all over Indonesia. As the young Obama was enjoying his childhood, the greatest Indonesian writer—Pramoedya Ananta Toer—wrote that the rivers were clogged with human corpses. The military regime and sympathetic right-wing religious cadres murdered 40 percent of Javanese teachers and the military was substituting in classes. It is hard to imagine the horror of post-1965 Indonesia. Yet, President Obama has warm memories about those years.

NOAM CHOMSKY

How old was he? Was he old enough to know?

ANDRE VLTCHEK

He was a school-age kid, but even they would know. People were disappearing everywhere. There was no way to escape this. In those days, Indonesia had only around 100 million inhabitants; 2–3 percent of the population was murdered. Further millions were purged, raped, tortured, imprisoned. It would take great discipline not to notice and not to remember.

NOAM CHOMSKY

Does he mention anything about it?

ANDRE VLTCHEK

He mentioned something abstract, but he's mostly talking about his wonderful childhood in Jakarta, which makes one wonder whether the Republicans should really worry too much about him. I think he's quite a solid part of their establishment. His policies towards certain parts of the world—from Honduras to Indonesia—are very right wing and that is an under-statement.

NOAM CHOMSKY

I would say they are mainstream liberal, which is pretty far to the right.

ANDRE VLTCHEK

When his Secretary of State, Hillary Clinton, came to Jakarta, she said (and I am paraphrasing): "If somebody asks me whether Islam and democracy and women's rights can go hand in hand I would tell them go to Indonesia."

NOAM CHOMSKY

Suharto came to the U.S. in 1995. The Clinton administration welcomed him and described him as "our kind of guy." They knew what had happened in Indonesia. They knew about East Timor, they knew about the horror stories, and yet he is "our kind of guy." He opened up the society to Western investment and exploitation, so what's the problem?

ANDRE VLTCHEK

You are right: What's the problem…?

As we are coming to the end of our conversation, I would like to mention one topic that we did not touch on and which is so essential to all that we have mentioned before. It is interesting how complacent the American voter or European voter is.

I always notice that when I go to Germany, or England, or France, to a café and talk and listen to the people, they seem to be totally disillusioned with their political and social system. They don't like any of the political parties; they don't even really want to participate in the system. You hear it all the time, but then elections come and they vote either for the mainstream, i.e. right-wing candidates, or they choose extremist right wingers, as they periodically do in France. Some say they "punish" the system, but in reality voters punish themselves, and especially the rest of the world, which is forced to sustain still high standards of living of Western nations through plundering its own resources and other terrible means.

José Saramago wrote a brilliant novel called *Seeing* which is about what would happen to a "democratic" Western country where the majority of people begin spoiling their election ballot papers. The state declares martial law and basically starts killing its own citizens. So from his point of view, "democracy" in the West is allowed to function as long as it serves the interest of the ruling elites. People are allowed to go and vote, as long as they take the process seriously and actually do go to election booths and stick the paper in the box; and as long as they vote for the candidates that are supportive of the system. But in the moment when people refuse or reject the regime's perception of what democracy should be, the mechanism of brutality and oppression will kick in.

NOAM CHOMSKY

There is a famous line I think from Emma Goldman, "If voting changed anything, they'd make it illegal." Actually I had an interesting conversation about this with Lula [Luiz Inácio Lula da Silva] back in the late 1990s, before he was elected President.

I was in Brazil and I'd spent a fair amount of time with him. At that time his popularity was running very high in the polls and I asked him whether he thought he'd ever be elected. And he said, "I understand the mentality of the peasants and even if they support me, when they go into a voting booth they are going to ask themselves, 'could the country be run by someone like me?' And they will say, 'no, no, it's got to be run by those rich smart guys,' so they will vote for one of them." But this turned out to be wrong—the mentality changed.

ANDRE VLTCHEK

Noam, I would like to end our conversation here. We have addressed crimes against humanity committed by the United States, Europe and its allies after World War II. We are living through a very unsettling time. There are mass extermination campaigns taking place in Congo and Papua. Entire nations are being ravished: Somalia, Sudan, Uganda, Libya, and Afghanistan. There is a serious danger that some countries like Syria and Iran may be the next on the hit list. The West is often manufacturing conflicts, pushing countries to confrontation as I witnessed recently in the Philippines, where some of their academics was explaining to me how the West is actually pitching Philippines and other countries of the region against China over the disputed islands. Warfare has moved away from man-to-man combat, and is now dominated by deadly missiles, bombing campaigns and by the latest terrible weapons: drones, which are synonymous with terrorism and absolute impunity—they kill without the invading nation having to risk its own soldiers. It is a one-sided war; a video game for one side, the horror of destroyed villages, murdered individuals and mutilated bodies for the other.

The West seems to be trying to consolidate its control over the world. Not much stands in its way, just a few determined countries and determined individuals. But, as history shows, that still may be sufficient to stop the terror, and to ensure that humanism will prevail.

NOAM CHOMSKY

There are two tendencies going on at the same time. An outside observer looking at the world would say that the primary trajectory is towards suicide, like running over a cliff. But another is towards growing opposition, and this has had some successes. There are changes even in the last 30 to 40 years, and significant ones. The question is, which of these trajectories will dominate?

If you want to be realistic, it doesn't look very hopeful, but we have only two choices: one is to say "it's hopeless, let's give up" and help make sure the worst will happen. And the other is to say "well, we would like to make things better, so we will try." If it works, it works, if it doesn't, we go back to the worst choice. Those are the options for us.

Timeline

Compiled by Gabriel Humberstone

August 1945   The U.S. drops the first atomic bombs on Hiroshima and Nagasaki, killing an estimated 246,000 people. Six days later Japan surrenders to the Allies, ending World War II.

October 1945   The United Nations is established, with the U.S., Britain, France, the USSR, and China in positions of primacy as permanent members of the Security Council.

1946–54   First Indochina War: France fights the communist Viêt Minh in an attempt to regain colonial control of Vietnam, which was occupied by Japan during World War II. By the end of the war the French have left Southeast Asia, and Vietnam is partitioned into the Communist North and the U.S.-supported South.

1947–48   First Kashmir War fought between India and Pakistan over disputed territories Kashmir and Jammu. It was the first of four wars between the nations over the territories.

April 1949   Formation of the North Atlantic Treaty Organization, NATO, bringing together key political and military powers in a mutual defense agreement and entrenched U.S. power over much of the globe.

July 1953   Arab nationalist coup in Iraq, known as the 14 July Revolution, which overthrows the British-backed Hashemite monarchy.

August 1953   Iranian coup orchestrated by the United States and Britain. Democratically elected prime minister

	Mohammad Mosaddegh is replaced by a military government under Mohammad Rezā Shāh Pahlavī.
June 1954	CIA-backed coup in Guatemala known as Operation PBFORTUNE. The president Jacobo Árbenz Guzmán is ousted and replaced by a military junta headed by Colonel Carlos Castillo.
January 1959	Cuban Revolution. Following growing hostility to the revolutionary government from the U.S., Cuba develops ties with the USSR.
February 1961	Assassination of Patrice Lumumba, the first democratically elected prime minister of the Republic of the Congo, by the U.S. and UK.
August 1961	The U.S. trials chemical warfare on Vietnam with the substance known as Agent Orange. In November President Kennedy signs the Foreign Assistance Act, providing "assistance to countries threatened by communism." U.S. military involvement in Southeast Asia gradually escalates.
October 1962	The Cuban missile crisis. Thirteen days of escalating tension between the U.S. and the USSR as the latter attempts to install nuclear missiles on Cuban soil in an effort to stop further attempts at U.S. invasion. In the end, the USSR backs down after the U.S. agrees to remove some missiles from Turkey and Italy.
March 1964	Brazilian coup leading to the overthrow of President João Goulart. The military regime that takes control is closely aligned with the U.S. government.
1964–73	Bombing of the Plain of Jars in Laos by the U.S. as the war in Southeast Asia escalates. The most intensive bombing campaign in U.S. history; more bombs are dropped here than during World War II.
1965	Attempted coup in Indonesia, backed by the U.S. The coup fails and is blamed on the Communist Party. Following this, between 500,000 and three million people are killed in an anti-Communist purge. President Sukarno is removed and soon

replaced by General Suharto, whose oppressive military regime is backed by the U.S.

1966–88 Namibian War of Independence. Cuba supports the Southwest Africa People's Organization (SWAPO) militarily, economically and politically. Two thousand Cuban fighters die in the 22-year conflict.

1967–74 Military dictatorship of Greece following a coup led by a group of right-wing military officers.

August 1968 Soviet invasion of Czechoslovakia, following the period of political liberalization under Alexander Dubček, known as the Prague Spring.

1969–70 Operation Menu carpet-bombing campaign on eastern Cambodia and Laos by the United States, targeting Vietnamese Communists.

September 1973 U.S.-sponsored coup against President Allende of Chile.

1975–91 Western Saharan War. After Spanish withdrawal from Morocco, the army takes control of the Western Sahara. The Polisario Front of the Sahrawi people fight for independence from Morocco; the dispute is still ongoing.

1975 Cuba intervenes to support the Peoples Movement for the Liberation of Angola against U.S.-backed intervention from South Africa and Zaire.

December 1975 Indonesia invades East Timor, leaving the country under occupation until 1999. An estimated 100,000–180,000 are killed during the conflict and occupation.

1978–82 Rio Negre Massacre in Guatemala. With funding from the World Bank and Inter American Development Bank, the Guatemalan government begins construction on the Chixoy Hydroelectric Dam forcing thousands of Maya Achi people off the land. Up to 5,000 people are killed during the expropriation.

1979–92	Salvadoran civil war. Conflict between the U.S.-backed military government against a coalition of left-wing guerrilla groups. The United States has as yet paid no reparations for the violence they funded.
April 1986	Bombing of Libya by the U.S. (Operation El Dorado Canyon).
November 1988	The U.S. fully adopts the UN Genocide convention; since its creation in 1948 it had been granted immunity from prosecution.
June 1989	Tiananmen Square massacre. Demonstrations in China after the death of reformer Zhao Ziyang leads to a crackdown in which protestors are fired upon by the military. The exact number of dead is not known. It was proven that the West, to destabilize China, directly funded many protesters.
September 1989	U.S. invasion of Panama, code-named Operation Just Cause. An estimated 3,500 people are killed.
November 1989	Fall of the Berlin Wall: Emblematic moment in the collapse of Communist regimes in Eastern Europe which was ongoing throughout 1989.
	Murder of Six Jesuit priests including Oscar Romero in San Salvador by the Atlacatl brigade of the El Salvadorian army. This was one of the bloodiest moments of the Salvadoran Civil War.
1990	Iraq–Kuwait war leading to Iraq's annexation of Kuwait and the First Gulf War.
	South African President F.W. de Klerk releases Nelson Mandela and begins negotiations that bring an end to the Apartheid regime in South Africa.
1991	Dissolution of the USSR under Mikhail Gorbachev, formally ending the Cold War.
April 1994	Downing of presidential plane in 1994 over Kigali in which Hutu presidents of Rwanda and Burundi died, leading to the Rwandan genocide and the consequent genocide in DR Congo, in which between four and ten million people are still dying,

as both Rwanda and Uganda plunder the country on behalf of Western companies and governments.

February 1999   Hugo Chavez wins elections in Venezuela, signaling the beginning of the so-called "pink tide" in Latin America and the end of the Washington Consensus that dominated South American politics during the 1990s.

March–June 1999   NATO bombing campaign on Belgrade ending the Kosovo conflict. Yugoslavia later unsuccessfully attempts to bring a case against NATO for the bombing.

October 2001   Start of U.S.-led invasion of Afghanistan following the terrorist attacks of September 11, 2001.

April 2002   Failed coup by members of the Venezuelan military. The U.S. is quick to acknowledge the legitimacy of the new government but switches once Chavez returns to office after only 47 hours.

August 2002   U.S. signs American Service Members' protection pact, the Hague Invasion Act that safeguards it from being prosecuted in any international court of which the U.S. is not a member.

March 2003   Start of the second Iraq war.

February 2004   Coup in Haiti in which the serving president Jean- Bernard Aristide is forced into exile in South Africa. It is widely acknowledged that the coup was orchestrated in part by the U.S. government.

June 2004   First known U.S. attack on Pakistan using unarmed drone planes in an attempt to target Taliban and Al Qaida forces. An estimated 366 strikes have taken place since.

2005   Cuba offers medical support to the U.S. following Hurricane Katrina. The aid was rejected by the U.S. State Department.

March 2006   Michelle Bachelet Jeria is sworn in as the first female president of Chile. A longtime socialist, she was at one time tortured under the U.S.-supported Pinochet regime.

May 2008	The Union of South American Nations (UNASUR) is formed signaling increased cooperation between South American states.
June 2009	The Honduran military ousts President Manuel Zelaya. Internationally acknowledged as a coup, every country in the region barring the U.S. withdraws its ambassadors.
May 2010	A flotilla bringing humanitarian aid and construction materials to Gaza from Turkey is intercepted and attacked by the Israeli Defense Force; nine activists are killed. In response Turkey recalled its ambassador in Israel and cancels joint military exercises.
December 2010	Protests start in Tunisia following the self-immolation of a protester outside a governor's office. The event catalyzed the Tunisian revolution, which then sparked off a region-wide revolutionary wave known as the Arab Spring.
2011	International military intervention into Libya during the civil war. There was little support for intervention outside of Britain, France, and the United States.
December 2011	The Community of Latin American and Caribbean States, CELAC, is founded, formally excluding the U.S. and Canada it provides an alternative to the Washington dominated Organization of American States (OAS).
August 2012	UN General Assembly passes a resolution against the Assad-led Syrian government. Russia, China, Brazil, India, and South Africa opposed what they saw as blatant support for the opposition.

Index

Compiled by Sue Carlton

Page numbers in **bold** refer to photographs